ASVAB
SUCCESS

ASVAB SUCCESS

2nd Edition

Copyright © 2006 LearningExpress, LLC.

All rights reserved under International and Pan-American Copyright Conventions.
Published in the United States by LearningExpress, LLC, New York.

Library of Congress Cataloging-in-Publication Data:
ASVAB success.—2nd ed.
   p. cm.
 ISBN 1-57685-543-0
 1. Armed Services Vocational Aptitude Battery—Study guides. 2. United States—Armed Forces—
Examinations. I. LearningExpress (Organization) II. Title.
U408.5.A847 2006
355.00973—dc22

                                                                           2006040833

Printed in the United States of America

9 8 7 6 5 4 3 2 1

Second Edition

ISBN 1-57685-543-0

For information on LearningExpress, other LearningExpress products, or bulk sales, please write to us at:
  LearningExpress
  55 Broadway
  8th Floor
  New York, NY 10006

Or visit us at:
  www.learnatest.com

Contents

SECTION 1 Preparing for the ASVAB — 1
    Lesson 1 About the ASVAB — 3
    Lesson 2 The LearningExpress Test Preparation System — 11
    Lesson 3 Multiple-Choice Test Strategies — 27

SECTION 2 Math for the Arithmetic Reasoning and Mathematics Knowledge Subtests — 33
    Lesson 4 Basic Arithmetic Functions — 37
    Lesson 5 Fractions, Decimals, Percents, and Averages — 47
    Lesson 6 Geometry and Algebra — 71
    Lesson 7 Word Problems — 81

SECTION 3 Reading Comprehension for the Paragraph Comprehension Subtest — 89
    Lesson 8 Reading Comprehension Basics — 93
    Lesson 9 Structure — 103
    Lesson 10 Language and Style — 113
    Lesson 11 Drawing Conclusions — 123

SECTION 4 Vocabulary for the Word Knowledge Subtest — 131
    Lesson 12 Word Parts — 133
    Lesson 13 Words in Context — 143
    Lesson 14 Synonyms and Antonyms — 157

ASVAB SUCCESS

SECTION

Preparing for the ASVAB

EVERY PERSON WHO wants to enlist in the Army, Navy, Air Force, Marines, or Coast Guard must take the Armed Services Vocational Battery (ASVAB). If you are thinking about joining the military and have chosen this book to prepare for the ASVAB exam, you are a giant leap ahead of people who will take the ASVAB, but will not study for it.

To succeed on the ASVAB, you must prepare. That is because your ASVAB score not only determines if you can enlist, but also determines for which military jobs you will qualify. Make no mistake: The better you score on the ASVAB, the more job choices will be open to you.

To get you the score you need, Section 1 of *ASVAB Success, Second Edition* provides you with the most up-to-date information on the exam. You will also complete the exclusive nine-step LearningExpress Test Preparation System to minimize test stress and maximize your score. Finally, you will learn even more multiple-choice test strategies to give you the score you need for the career you want.

Now get started and good luck!

LESSON

About the ASVAB

The Armed Services Vocational Aptitude Battery, or ASVAB, is a multiple-aptitude test consisting of eight subtests on various subjects. The ASVAB is used for two main purposes:

- As a military recruiting tool of the U.S. Department of Defense to test potential recruits to determine their developed abilities (i.e., to gauge what they already know about certain subjects); to measure their general learning ability and vocational aptitude; and to predict performance in certain academic areas
- As a guide for high school and post-secondary school students, to help them decide upon career paths for which they might best be suited, whether in the military or in some other field

Before we go into greater detail about the exam, let's review the process of joining the military and some of the jobs that are available to you there.

ABOUT THE ASVAB

▶ Basic Requirements

Certain requirements must be met in order to enlist in any branch of the military. You must:

- be between 17 and 34 years of age and have a parent or guardian's permission if you are under the age of 18.
- be a U.S. citizen.
- have a high school diploma or GED.
- be drug-free.
- have a clean arrest record.

It is important to be truthful with your recruiter about any trouble you have had in the past with drugs or with the law. Criminal history checks are conducted on applicants. However, some kinds of problems can be overcome, if they are really *in the past*, not current difficulties. Check with your recruiter.

▶ Working with Your Recruiter

The recruiter is there to help you. In speaking with him or her, you will have the opportunity to ask as many questions as you want and get a detailed picture of what each branch has to offer. All recruiters will have brochures, videotapes, pamphlets, and years of personal experience to offer as resources. Don't be afraid to bring along a parent or trusted friend to help you ask questions.

You can ask about salaries, fringe benefits, postings, and educational opportunities—including financial aid for college. The recruiter will also ask about you: your education, physical and mental health, and all sorts of in-depth questions about your goals, interests, hobbies, and life experience.

Your recruiter will talk to you about the benefits of enlisting: the pay, travel, experience, and training. You and your recruiter can also start to discuss the kinds of military jobs available. These jobs are mentioned later in this lesson.

▶ Military Entrance Processing Station (MEPS)

If you show definite interest in enlisting, your recruiter will schedule you for a trip to a MEPS in your area (there is one in almost every state) for a day of written and physical testing. The MEPS is where applicants for every branch of the military begin the enlistment process.

During your day at MEPS, you will go through three phases:

- **mental (aptitude) testing**—taking the ASVAB
- **medical exam**—having a routine physical by non-military doctors
- **administrative procedures**—filling out paperwork and discussing your military job options

If all three phases are successful, you will join the military and begin your Basic Training.

▶ Military Occupational Specialties (MOSs)

Joining the military does not just make you a soldier. In fact, there are numerous jobs and job types in every branch of the military. Here is a limited list of the many options available. Your score on some sections of the ASVAB *can* affect whether you are qualified to fill certain positions.

Administrative
Administrative Specialist
Cartographer
Executive Administrative Assistant
Finance Specialist
Information Systems Operator
Intelligence Analyst
Personnel Administration Specialist

The ASVAB for Non-Military Types

It's important to remember that taking the ASVAB does not obligate you to join the military. If you take the ASVAB with no intention of entering the military, the test is, for you, simply an aptitude test. Your results will help you determine if you have the aptitude for certain skills or whether you should seek additional training.

There is no cost for taking the ASVAB, and they are offered in recruitment centers and at some high schools. Recruiters or guidance counselors can explain your score report and how to use it.

Combat Specialty
Ammunition Specialist
Combat Engineer
Infantryman
M1 Armor (tank) Crewmember
PATRIOT Missile Crewmember

Construction
Carpentry and Masonry Specialist

Electronic and Electrical Equipment Repair
Radio Repairer

Engineering, Science, and Technical
Interior Electrician
Single Channel Radio Operator

Healthcare
Animal Care Specialist
Behavioral Science Specialist
Dental Laboratory Specialist
Medical Specialist
Practical Nurse
Psychological Operations Specialist
X-Ray Specialist

Machine Operator and Precision Work
Crane Operator
Machinist

Media and Public Affairs
Broadcast Journalist
Multimedia Illustrator

Transportation and Material Handling
Fabric Repair Specialist
Motor Transport Operator
Watercraft Operator

Vehicle and Machinery Mechanic
Aviation Systems Repairer
Light-Wheel Vehicle Mechanic
PATRIOT System Repairer
UH-60 Helicopter Repairer

Do any of these jobs interest you? Keep in mind that if you want to qualify to fill these positions, you have to receive a specified minimum score on different sections on the ASVAB.

Now it's time to review the ASVAB in greater detail so you know exactly what you will face on test day and what you will have to study to get the score you need.

▶ More Information on the ASVAB

Depending on where you take the ASVAB, you will take either the computer version or the paper-and-pencil version. Candidates for enlistment taking the ASVAB at a MEPS will take the computer version, while

ABOUT THE ASVAB

candidates for enlistment taking the ASVAB at a reserve center or Mobile Examination Team (MET) site will take the paper-and-pencil version. The content of the test is the same on both versions; only the format, the mechanics of scoring, and the number of questions asked are slightly different.

NUMBER OF ITEMS AND TESTING TIME FOR THE ASVAB

Subtest	Number of Questions	Time (Minutes)
General Science (GS)	25	11
Arithmetic Reasoning (AR)	30	36
Word Knowledge (WK)	25	11
Paragraph Comprehension (PC)	15	13
Auto and Shop Information (AS)	25	11
Mathematics Knowledge (MK)	35	24
Mechanical Comprehension (MC)	25	19
Electronics Information (EI)	20	9
Total	**200 Items**	**134 Minutes**

Most sections of the ASVAB—General Science, Arithmetic Reasoning, Word Knowledge, Auto and Shop Information, Mathematics Knowledge, Mechanical Comprehension, and Electronics Information—depend on your knowing about the subject from your high school courses or other reading.

The one section that does not depend on previous knowledge is the Paragraph Comprehension section. For these questions, you will find the answers using only the information given in the paragraph.

▶ The Eight ASVAB Subtests

Following is a more detailed description of each of the eight subtests in the ASVAB.

Part 1: General Science

The General Science subtest of the ASVAB consists of 25 questions that are designed to measure your ability to recognize, apply, and analyze basic scientific principles in the areas of:

- **Life science**—botany, zoology, anatomy and physiology, ecology
- **Physical Science**—force and motion, energy, fluids and gases, atomic structure, chemistry
- **Earth and space science**—astronomy, geology, meteorology, oceanography

Here is a sample General Science question, followed by its answer.

1. Substances that speed up reaction time without undergoing changes themselves are called
   a. buffers.
   b. colloids.
   c. reducers.
   d. catalysts.

The answer is **d**.

Part 2: Arithmetic Reasoning

The Arithmetic Reasoning subtest consists of 30 word problems describing everyday life situations. The questions are designed to measure your reasoning skills and understanding of:

- Operations with whole numbers
- Operations with fractions and decimals or money
- Ratio and proportion
- Interest and percentage
- Measurement of perimeters, areas, volumes, and time and temperature

Here is a sample Arithmetic Reasoning question, followed by its answer.

1. If 12 men are needed to run four machines, how many men are needed to run 20 machines?
   a. 20
   b. 48
   c. 60
   d. 80

   The answer is **c**.

Part 3: Word Knowledge

The Word Knowledge subtest consists of 25 questions that ask you to choose the correct definition of verbs, nouns, adjectives, and adverbs. These questions come in two forms:

- Definitions presented alone, with no context
- Words in the context of a short sentence

Here is a sample Word Knowledge question, followed by its answer.

1. *Rudimentary* most nearly means
   a. political.
   b. minute.
   c. promotional.
   d. basic.

   The answer is **d**.

Part 4: Paragraph Comprehension

The Paragraph Comprehension subtest is 15 questions based on several short passages written on a variety of topics. No prior knowledge of the subject is required—all the information you will need to answer the questions will be found in the passage. The questions are designed to test your ability to obtain the following kinds of information from written material:

- **Literal comprehension**—your ability to identify stated facts, identify reworded facts, and determine the sequence of events
- **Implicit, inferential, or critical comprehension**—your ability to draw conclusions; identify the main idea of a paragraph; determine the author's purpose, mood, or tone; and identify style and technique

Here is a sample Paragraph Comprehension question, followed by its answer.

1. In certain areas, water is so scarce that every attempt is made to conserve it. For instance, on an oasis in the Sahara Desert, the amount of water necessary for each date palm has been carefully determined.

    How much water is each tree likely to be given?
    a. no water at all
    b. water on alternate days
    c. exactly the amount required
    d. water only if it is a young tree

    The answer is **c**.

Part 5: Auto and Shop Information

The Auto and Shop Information subtest includes 25 questions on automotive repair and building construction. General shop practices are also included. The questions cover the following topics:

- Automotive components
- Automotive systems
- Automotive tools
- Automotive troubleshooting and repair
- Shop tools
- Building materials
- Building and construction procedures

Here is a sample Auto and Shop Information question, followed by its answer.

1. A chisel is used for
    a. drilling
    b. cutting
    c. twisting
    d. grinding

    The answer is **b**.

Part 6: Mathematics Knowledge

The Mathematics Knowledge subtest consists of 35 questions designed to measure your understanding of mathematical concepts, principles, and procedures. The emphasis is on your ability to recognize and apply basic mathematical principles. The questions cover:

- **Number theory**—factors, multiples, reciprocals, number properties, primes, integers
- **Numeration**—fractional parts, decimals, percentages, and conversions; order of operations; exponents; rounding; reducing fractions; roots and radicals; signed numbers
- **Algebraic operations and equations**—solving or determining equations, factoring, simplifying algebraic expressions, converting a sentence to an equation
- **Geometry and measurement**—coordinates and slope, angle measurement, properties of polygons and circles, perimeter, area, volume, unit conversion
- **Probability**—the likelihood of the outcomes of certain events

Here is a sample Mathematics Knowledge question, followed by its answer.

1. If 50% of $x = 66$, then x equals?
    a. 33
    b. 66
    c. 99
    d. 132

    The answer is **d**.

Part 7: Mechanical Comprehension

The Mechanical Comprehension subtest consists of 25 questions, many of them illustrated, on general mechanics and physical principles. The questions cover simple machines, including gears, pulleys, and levers; as well as force and fluid dynamics. Problems involving basic properties of materials are also included. The questions may consist of knowledge, application, and analysis questions covering:

- **Basic compound machines**—gears, cams, pistons, cranks, linkages, belts, chains
- **Simple machines**—levers, pulleys, screws, wedges, wheels, axles
- **Mechanical motion**—friction, velocity, direction, acceleration, centrifugal force
- **Fluid dynamics**—hydraulic forces, compression
- **Properties of materials**—weight, strength, expansion/contraction, absorption, density
- **Structural support**—center of gravity, weight distribution

Here is a sample Mechanical Comprehension question, followed by its answer.

1. An elevator uses which of the following mechanical devices?
   a. a cable
   b. a pulley
   c. a motor
   d. all of the above

The answer is **d**.

Part 8: Electronics Information

The Electronics Information subtest consists of 20 questions on electrical and electronic systems. These questions are designed to measure basic knowledge and principles of electrical and electronic systems including:

- Electrical tools, symbols, devices, and materials
- Electrical circuits
- Electricity and electronic systems
- Electrical current: voltage, conductivity, resistance, and grounding

Here is a sample Electronics Information question, followed by its answer.

1. In electrical terms, what does the abbreviation AC stand for?
   a. additional charge
   b. alternating coil
   c. alternating current
   d. ampere current

The answer is **c**.

Now that we have reviewed the subtests of the ASVAB, it is time to address the Armed Forces Qualifying Test (AFQT).

▶ The Armed Forces Qualifying Test (AFQT)

Although eight subtests comprise the entire ASVAB, only four of these subtests are used to determine whether you can enlist in the military. Only your scores on the Arithmetic Reasoning, Word Knowledge, Paragraph Comprehension, and Mathematics Knowledge subtests count toward your AFQT score. Simply put, if your AFQT score is not above a passing level, you will not be able to enlist. That is why it is critically important to pass each of these subtests, sometimes referred to as the ASVAB Core, to ensure that you can enlist.

In case you are wondering, the other four subtests—General Science, Auto and Shop Information, Mechanical Comprehension, and Electronics Information help determine for which jobs you are suited. Even if you have a passing AFQT score and are able to enlist, you should aim to do your best on these other subtests to improve your chances of obtaining the job you want.

▶ How This Book Can Help You

The lessons in the rest of Section 1 offer you tips and strategies for doing your best on any test you take. On the other hand, the lessons found in Sections 2, 3, and 4 of this book provide you with targeted information and strategies to improve your basic reading, math, and vocabulary skills to get a top score on ASVAB subtests.

While studying the math lessons, you will:

- Review basic operations such as addition, subtraction, multiplication, and division
- Get ready to tackle fractions, decimals, percents, and word problems
- Gain a working knowledge of basic geometry, including lines, angles, triangles, rectangles, squares, and circles
- Refresh your knowledge of math terms

In the reading comprehension lessons, you will learn to:

- Find important facts while reading
- Locate main ideas
- Sort out fact from opinion
- Understand tools used by writers such as language choice and structure

Finally, the vocabulary lessons will help you:

- Use root words to discover word meanings
- Define and use common word prefixes and suffixes
- Figure out unfamiliar words using context

Also, be sure to complete the practice questions found in each lesson, so you can determine which areas you have mastered and which still need more work.

LESSON 2 ▶ The LearningExpress Test Preparation System

Taking the ASVAB demands a lot of preparation if you want to achieve a passing score. Your future depends on passing the exam. The LearningExpress Test Preparation System, developed exclusively for LearningExpress by leading test experts, gives you the discipline and attitude required to achieve winning results.

Before we cover all the ways you can succeed on this exam, let's review some of the pitfalls that can keep you from your top score:

- being unfamiliar with the format and content of the exam
- having high levels of test anxiety
- leaving your preparation to the last minute
- not preparing at all
- not knowing crucial test-taking skills, such as how to pace yourself through the exam, how to use the process of elimination, and when to guess
- not being in the mental and physical shape required to complete the exam
- arriving late at the exam site, having to work on an empty stomach, or shivering through the exam because the room is cold

THE LEARNINGEXPRESS TEST PREPARATION SYSTEM

What is the reason for all of these test-taking pitfalls? Control. The LearningExpress Test Preparation System puts *you* in control. In nine easy-to-follow steps, you will learn everything you need to know to ensure that you are in charge of your preparation and your performance on the exam. By completing this chapter, you will have taken all the needed steps to achieve a high score on the ASVAB.

The LearningExpress Test Preparation System works through nine easy steps, which lead you through everything you need to know and do to prepare for this or any exam. Each of the following steps includes both reading about the step and one activity. It's important that you do the activities along with the reading, or you won't be getting the full benefit of the system. Each step tells you approximately how much time that step will take you to complete.

Step 1: Learn About the Exam	50 minutes
Step 2: Combat Test Anxiety	20 minutes
Step 3: Create a Study Plan	30 minutes
Step 4: Learn to Manage Your Time	10 minutes
Step 5: Practice the Process of Elimination	20 minutes
Step 6: Understand When to Guess	20 minutes
Step 7: Prepare for Peak Performance	10 minutes
Step 8: Make Final Test-Day Preparations	10 minutes
Step 9: Ace the Exam!	10 minutes
Total	**3 hours**

We estimate the entire system in this chapter will take approximately three hours. If you prefer, you can complete the whole LearningExpress Test Preparation System in one sitting. Otherwise, you can do just one or two steps per day for the next several days. It's up to you—remember, *you* are in control.

▶ Step 1: Learn about the Exam

Time to complete: 50 minutes
Activity: Read Lesson 1, "About the ASVAB"
Knowing what to expect on test day accomplishes several things. First, it lowers your test anxiety, because you can anticipate the kinds of questions asked. Also, knowing what is being tested helps you prepare and focus your study time. For these reasons, the first step in the LearningExpress Test Preparation System is finding out everything you can about the ASVAB.

Why Do You Have to Take This Exam, Anyway?

It's important for you to remember that your score on the ASVAB does not determine the kind of person you are or even whether or not you will make a good serviceperson. An exam like this can't test whether you can follow orders; whether you can become part of a unit that works together to accomplish a task; and so on. Those kinds of things are hard to measure, while a test is easy to evaluate.

THE LEARNINGEXPRESS TEST PREPARATION SYSTEM

However, your chances of getting into the military *still* depend on your getting a good score on the subtests of the ASVAB, and that's why you are here—using the LearningExpress Test Preparation System to achieve control over the exam.

Test Content and Format

If you haven't done so, stop here and read Lesson 1 of this book, which gives you an overview of the ASVAB. Once you have your information, the next steps in the LearningExpress Test Preparation System will show you what to do with it.

▶ Step 2: Combat Test Anxiety

Time to complete: 20 minutes
Activity: Take the Test Stress Questionnaire

Knowing what is being tested and the types of questions asked is the first step toward gaining control of the exam. Next, you have to overcome one of the biggest obstacles to test success: test anxiety. Test anxiety not only impairs your performance on the exam itself; but also keeps you from preparing. In this step, you will learn stress management techniques that will help you succeed on your exam. However, don't expect to read through and master these techniques in one sitting.

Test Stress Questionnaire

In general, you only need to worry about test anxiety if it is extreme enough to impair your performance. The following questions will provide an informal diagnosis of your level of test anxiety. In the blank before each statement, write the number that most accurately describes your experience.

0 = Never   1 = Once or twice   2 = Sometimes   3 = Often

_____ I have gotten so nervous before an exam that I simply put down the books and didn't study for it.

_____ I have experienced physical symptoms such as vomiting and severe headaches because I was nervous about an exam.

_____ I have simply not showed up for an exam because I was scared.

_____ I have experienced dizziness and disorientation while taking an exam.

_____ I have had trouble filling in the little circles because my hands were shaking too hard.

_____ I have failed an exam because I was too nervous to complete it.

_____ **Total: Add up the numbers in the blanks.**

Your Test Stress Score

Here are the steps you should take, depending on your score. If you scored:

- **Below 3,** your level of test anxiety is nothing to worry about; it's probably just enough to keep you driven to do your best.
- **Between 3 and 6,** your test anxiety may be enough to impair your performance, and you should practice the stress management techniques listed in this step of the LearningExpress Test Preparation System to try to lower your test anxiety to more manageable levels.
- **Above 6,** your level of test anxiety is a concern. In addition to practicing the stress management techniques listed in this step, you may want to work with a tutor or academic counselor to combat your anxiety.

THE LEARNINGEXPRESS TEST PREPARATION SYSTEM

You will need to practice them as you practice the exams in this book, so that they will come naturally to you on test day.

The Test Anxiety Edge

It is important to understand that a little test anxiety is a good thing. Everyone gets nervous before a big exam—and if that nervousness motivates you to prepare thoroughly and stay focused on your goal, so much the better. In fact, some test anxiety gives you a little extra edge—just the kind of edge you need to do well.

On page 13 is the Test Stress Questionnaire. Stop here and answer the questions to find out whether or not your level of test anxiety is enough to provide you an edge.

Stress Management before the Test

To keep your stress level at a reasonable minimum, we suggest the following:

- **Get prepared.** There's nothing like knowing what to expect and being prepared for it to put you in control of test anxiety. This book will help you prepare and get the score you need.
- **Practice self-confidence.** A positive attitude is a great way to combat test anxiety. Don't be shy. Stand in front of the mirror and say to your reflection, "I am prepared. I am full of self-confidence. I am going to ace this test. I know I can do it." Say it once a day. If you hear it often enough, you will believe it.
- **Ignore negative messages.** Every time someone starts telling you how hard the exam is or how it's almost impossible to get a high score, start telling them your self-confidence messages. Don't listen to the negative messages. Repeat your self-confidence messages.
- **Visualize.** Imagine putting on your new uniform and beginning your first day of Basic Training. Visualizing success can help make it happen—and it reminds you of why you are going to this effort to prepare for the exam.

- **Exercise.** Physical activity helps relieve stress and focus your mind. Go for a run, lift weights, go swimming—and do it regularly. Being in good physical shape can actually help you do well on the exam.

Stress Management on Test Day

There are several ways you can lower your test anxiety on test day. They work best if you practice them in the weeks before the test, so you know which ones work best for you.

- **Breathe deeply.** Take a deep breath while you count to five. Hold it for a count of one, then let it out on a count of five. Repeat several times.
- **Move your body.** Try rolling your head in a circle. Rotate your shoulders. Shake your hands from the wrist. Many people find these movements very relaxing.
- **Visualize a relaxing place.** Think of the place where you are most relaxed: lying on the beach in the sun, walking through the park, or whatever. Now close your eyes and imagine you are actually there. If you practice in advance, you will find that you only need a few seconds of this exercise to experience a significant increase in your sense of well-being.

Stress Management during the Test

If anxiety threatens to overwhelm you during the exam, there are still things you can do to manage the stress level:

- **Repeat your self-confidence messages.** You should have them memorized by now. Say them silently to yourself, and believe them.
- **Visualize completing the test.** This time, visualize yourself moving smoothly and quickly through the test, answering every question correctly and finishing early. Like most visualization techniques, this one works best if you have practiced it ahead of time.
- **Find an easy question.** Find an easy question, and answer it. Finishing even one question helps boost

THE LEARNINGEXPRESS TEST PREPARATION SYSTEM

your sense of accomplishment and self-confidence.
- **Take a mental break.** Everyone loses concentration once in a while during a test. It's normal, so you shouldn't worry about it. Instead, accept what has happened. Say to yourself, "Hey, I lost it there for a minute. My brain is taking a break." Put down your pencil, close your eyes, and do some deep breathing for a few seconds. Then you are ready to go back to work.

Remember, do not attempt these techniques for the first time on test day. Try them while studying or taking the practice tests in this book.

▶ Step 3: Create a Study Plan

Time to complete: 30 minutes
Activity: Construct and follow a study schedule
Maybe the most important thing you can do to get control of yourself and your exam is to make a study plan. Too many people don't plan ahead and instead spend hours the day before the exam staring at lessons and sample questions. This method only raises your level of test anxiety, and does not substitute for careful preparation and practice.

So don't wait until the last minute and cram. Take control of your preparation time by planning ahead and making a study schedule. On the following pages you will find three sample schedules, based on the amount of time you may have before you take the ASVAB. These may work for you, but don't be afraid to construct your own or to adapt them to your schedule. Be honest about how much time you have to study, and don't give up if you fall behind schedule. If something unforeseen delays your studying, make up for it when you have time.

Even more important than making a plan is making a commitment. You can't review everything you need to know for the exam in one night. You have to set aside time every day for study and practice. Shoot for at least 30 minutes a day. Thirty minutes daily is more effective than three hours on Saturday.

Schedule A: The One-Month Plan
If you have at least a month before you take the ASVAB, you have plenty of time to prepare, but don't waste it. If you have less than a month, turn to Schedule B.

TIME	PREPARATION
Days 1–4	Use these first days to learn about the exam and work through the LearningExpress Test Preparation System. Be sure you are prepared and committed to starting the studying process.
Days 5–11	Review Section 2: Math for the Arithmetic Reasoning and Mathematics Knowledge Subtests. Complete all practice questions.
Day 12	Review the answers to the practice questions. Go back and study the tips and strategies in Lessons 4, 5, 6, and 7.
Days 13–19	Review Section 3: Reading Comprehension for the Paragraph Comprehension Subtest. Complete all practice questions.
Day 20	Review the answers to the practice questions. Go back and study the tips and strategies in Lessons 8, 9, 10, and 11.

THE LEARNINGEXPRESS TEST PREPARATION SYSTEM

Days 21–26	Review Section 4: Vocabulary for the Word Knowledge Subtest. Complete all practice questions.
Day 27	Once again, review the answers to the practice questions. Go back and study the tips and strategies in Lessons 12, 13, and 14.
Days 28–29	Think about which skills are your weakest. Return to those lessons and review them more thoroughly.
Day before the exam	Relax. Do something unrelated to the exam, and go to bed at a reasonable hour.

Schedule B: The Two-Week Plan

If you have at least two weeks before you take the exam, use this schedule to help make the most of your time. If you have less than two weeks, turn to Schedule C.

TIME	PREPARATION
Day 1	Use the first day to learn about the exam and work through the LearningExpress Test Preparation System. Be sure you are prepared and committed to starting the studying process.
Days 2–4	Review Section 2: Math for the Arithmetic Reasoning and Mathematics Knowledge Subtests. Complete all practice questions.
Day 5	Review the answers to the practice questions. Go back and study the tips and strategies in Lessons 4, 5, 6, and 7.
Days 6–8	Review Section 3: Reading Comprehension for the Paragraph Comprehension Subtest. Complete all practice questions.
Day 9	Review the answers to the practice questions. Go back and study the tips and strategies in Lessons 8, 9, 10, and 11.
Days 10–12	Review Section 4: Vocabulary for the Word Knowledge Subtest. Complete all practice questions.
Day 13	Once again, review the answers to the practice questions. Go back and study the tips and strategies in Lessons 12, 13, and 14.
Day before the exam	Relax. Do something unrelated to the exam, and go to bed at a reasonable hour.

THE LEARNINGEXPRESS TEST PREPARATION SYSTEM

Schedule C: The One-Week Plan

If you have only one week before you take the exam, use this schedule to help make the most of your limited time. You will have to commit fully to preparing as best you can.

TIME	PREPARATION
Day 1	Spend some time learning about the exam and working through the LearningExpress Test Preparation System.
Day 2	Review Section 2: Math for the Arithmetic Reasoning and Mathematics Knowledge Subtests. Complete all practice questions.
Day 3	Review Section 3: Reading Comprehension for the Paragraph Comprehension Subtest. Complete all practice questions.
Day 4	Review Section 4: Vocabulary for the Word Knowledge Subtest. Complete all practice questions.
Days 5–6	Think about which skills are your weakest. Return to those lessons and review them more thoroughly.
Day before the exam	Use the first part of your last study day to review areas that are still giving you trouble. By the evening, you should stop studying and relax. Do something unrelated to the exam, and go to bed at a reasonable hour.

▶ Step 4: Learn to Manage Your Time

Time to complete: 10 minutes to read, many hours of practice!
Activity: Practice these strategies as you take the sample tests in this book

Steps 4, 5, and 6 of the LearningExpress Test Preparation System put you in charge of your exam by showing you test-taking strategies that work. Practice these strategies as you take the sample tests in this book, and you will be ready to use them on test day.

First, you will take control of your time on the exam. By doing this you will avoid a situation where there are only minutes left, and you are still far from finishing the exam.

- **Follow directions.** On test day, don't spend a lot of time reviewing the directions in detail. However, make sure you know exactly what you are required to do.
- **Pace yourself.** Whether you are taking the computer-based ASVAB or paper-based ASVAB, use a watch or clock to keep track of time.
- **Keep moving.** Don't waste time on one question. If you don't know the answer, skip the question and move on. You may be able to return to it later. All questions have the same point value. You should answer as many questions as you can rather than spending time answering one difficult question.
- **Don't rush.** Though you should keep moving, rushing won't help. Only careless errors and lost points come from rushing, so try to keep calm and work methodically and quickly.

THE LEARNINGEXPRESS TEST PREPARATION SYSTEM

▶ Step 5: Practice Process of Elimination

Time to complete: 20 minutes
Activity: Complete worksheet on Using the Process of Elimination

After time management, your next most important tool for taking control of your exam is using the process of elimination wisely. Standard test-taking wisdom dictates that you should always read all the answer choices before choosing your answer. This helps you find the right answer by eliminating incorrect answer choices.

Supposes you are facing an Electronics Information question that goes like this:

Which of the following has the least electrical resistence?
a. wood
b. iron
c. rubber
d. silver

Always use the process of elimination on a question like this, even if the right answer seems obvious.

Using the Process of Elimination

Use the process of elimination to answer the following questions.

1. Ilsa is as old as Meghan will be in five years. The difference between Ed's age and Meghan's age is twice the difference between Ilsa's age and Meghan's age. Ed is 29. How old is Ilsa?
   a. 4
   b. 10
   c. 19
   d. 24

2. "All drivers of commercial vehicles must carry a valid commercial driver's license whenever operating a commercial vehicle." According to this sentence, which of the following people need NOT carry a commercial driver's license?
   a. a truck driver idling the engine while waiting to be directed to a loading dock
   b. a bus operator backing a bus out of the way of another bus in the bus lot
   c. a taxi driver driving his or her personal car to the grocery store
   d. a limousine driver taking the limousine home after dropping off the last passenger of the evening

3. Smoking tobacco has been linked to
   a. increased risk of stroke and heart attack.
   b. all forms of respiratory disease.
   c. increasing mortality rates over the past ten years.
   d. juvenile delinquency.

4. Which of the following words is spelled correctly?
   a. incorrigible
   b. outragous
   c. domestickated
   d. understandible

18

Using the Process of Elimination (continued)

Answers

Here are the answers, as well as some suggestions as to how you might have used the process of elimination to find them.

1. **d.** You should have eliminated choice **a** immediately. Ilsa can't be four years old if Meghan is going to be Ilsa's age in five years. The best way to eliminate other answers is to try plugging them in to the information given in the problem. For instance, for choice **b**, if Ilsa is 10, then Meghan must be 5. The difference in their ages is 5. The difference between Ed's age, 29, and Meghan's age, 5, is 24. Is 24 two times 5? No. Then choice **b** is wrong. You could eliminate choice **c** in the same way and be left with choice **d**.

2. **c.** Note the word *not* in the question, and go through the answers one by one. Is the truck driver in choice **a** "operating a commercial vehicle"? Yes, idling counts as "operating," so he needs to have a commercial driver's license. Likewise, the bus operator in choice **b** is operating a commercial vehicle; the question doesn't say the operator has to be on the street. The limo driver in choice **d** is operating a commercial vehicle, even if it doesn't have passenger in it. However, the cab driver in choice **c** is *not* operating a commercial vehicle, but his or her own private car.

3. **a.** You could eliminate choice **b** simply because of the presence of the word *all*. Such absolutes hardly ever appear in correct answer choices. Choice **c** looks attractive until you think a little about what you know—aren't *fewer* people smoking these days, rather than more? So how could smoking be responsible for a higher mortality rate? (If you didn't know that *mortality rate* means the rate at which people die, you might keep this choice as a possibility, but you would still be able to eliminate two answers and have only two to choose from.) Choice **d** is not logical, so you could eliminate that one, too, leaving you with the correct choice, **a**.

4. **a.** How you used the process of elimination here depends on which words you recognized as spelled incorrectly. If you knew that the correct spellings were *outrageous*, *domesticated*, and *understandable*, then you were correct to choose **a**.

Sometimes the answer that jumps out isn't right after all. Let's assume, for the purpose of this exercise, that you are a little rusty on property electronics information, so you need to use some intuition to compensate for what you don't remember. Proceed through the answer choices in order.

So you start with choice **a**. This one is pretty easy to eliminate; wood has a fairly high resistance to electricity; make a mental note that answer choice **a** is incorrect.

Choice **b** seems reasonable; make a mental note, "Good answer, I might use this one."

Choice **c** strikes you as a less likely. Rubber has a fairly high resistance. Eliminate this one since you already found a choice (**c**) that is more reasonable.

Choice **d** is also a possibility. Make a mental note, "Good answer" or "Well, maybe," depending on how attractive this answer looks to you.

THE LEARNINGEXPRESS TEST PREPARATION SYSTEM

Now, since Electronics Information is a knowledge-based subtest, you will have to know that choice **b**, iron, is correct. However, using the process of elimination helped you narrow your choices down to only two.

If you take the ASVAB on paper, it's good to have a system for marking *good*, *bad*, and *maybe* answers. We are recommending this one:

X = bad
✔ = good
? = maybe

If you don't like these marks, devise your own system. Just make sure you do it long before test day, so you won't have to worry about it just before the exam.

Even when you think you are absolutely clueless about a question, you can often use process of elimination to discard at least one answer choice. If so, you are better prepared to make an educated guess, as you will see in Step 6. More often, the process of elimination allows you to get down to only two possible correct answers. Then you are in a stronger position to guess. Sometimes, even though you don't know the right answer, you find it simply by getting rid of the wrong ones, as you did in the previous example.

Try using these elimination skills on the questions in the Using the Process of Elimination worksheet. The questions are not sample ASVAB questions; they are just designed to show you how the process of elimination works. The answer explanations for this worksheet show one possible way you might use the process to arrive at the right answer.

The process of elimination is your tool for the next step: knowing when to guess.

▶ Step 6: Understand When to Guess

Time to complete: 20 minutes
Activity: Complete worksheet on Your Guessing Ability

Armed with the process of elimination, you are ready to take control of one of the big questions in test taking: Should I guess? The first and main answer is, yes. Some exams have a guessing penalty, in which a fraction of your incorrect answers is subtracted from your right answers—but the ASVAB doesn't work like that. The number of questions you answer correctly yields your raw score. So you have nothing to lose and everything to gain by guessing.

The more complicated answer to the question "Should I guess?" depends on you—your personality and your "guessing intuition." Ask yourself, "Am I a good guesser?"

To find out if you are a good guesser, complete the Your Guessing Ability worksheet that follows. Frankly, even if you have lousy intuition, you are still safe in guessing every time if there is no guessing penalty. The best thing would be to overcome your anxieties and mark an answer. But you may want to have a sense of how good your intuition is before you go into the exam.

▶ Step 7: Prepare for Peak Performance

Time to complete: 10 minutes to read, weeks to complete
Activity: Complete the Physical Preparation Checklist

To do your very best on an exam, you have to take control of your physical and mental state. Exercise, proper diet, and rest will ensure that your body works with, rather than against, your mind on exam day as well as during your preparation.

THE LEARNINGEXPRESS TEST PREPARATION SYSTEM

Exercise

If you don't already have an exercise routine, the time during which you are preparing for an exam is an excellent time to start one. You can incorporate your workouts into your study schedule. And if you are already keeping fit—or trying to get that way—don't let the pressure of preparing for an exam discourage your progress. Exercise helps reduce stress and increases the oxygen supply throughout your body, including your brain, so you will be at peak performance on exam day.

A half hour of vigorous activity—enough to raise a sweat—at least five times per week should be your aim. If you are pressed for time, three times per week should be the minimum. Most importantly, choose an activity you like and get out there and do it. Remember, moderation is the key. If you overdo it, you will only exhaust yourself.

Diet

The first, and perhaps the most difficult thing to do, is to cut out the junk. Chips, candy, and fast food will not improve your performance. Use caffeine only in moderation for at least two weeks before the exam.

There is never a good time to crash diet; instead what your body needs for peak performance is a

Your Guessing Ability

The following are five difficult questions. You are not supposed to know the answers. Rather, this is an assessment of your ability to guess when you don't have much information. Read each question carefully, just as if you did expect to answer it. If you have any knowledge at all of the subject of the question, use that knowledge to help you eliminate incorrrect answers.

1. September 7 is Independence Day in
   a. India.
   b. Costa Rica.
   c. Brazil.
   d. Australia.

2. American author Gertrude Stein was born in
   a. 1713.
   b. 1830.
   c. 1874.
   d. 1901.

3. The third Chief Justice of the U.S. Supreme Court was
   a. John Blair.
   b. William Cushing.
   c. James Wilson.
   d. John Jay.

4. Which of the following is the poisonous portion of a daffodil?
   a. the bulb
   b. the leaves
   c. the stem
   d. the flowers

5. The state with the highest per capita personal income in 1980 was
   a. Alaska.
   b. Connecticut.
   c. New York.
   d. Texas.

Your Guessing Ability (continued)

Answers
Check your answers against the following correct answers.

1. c.
2. c.
3. b.
4. a.
5. a.

The Results

How did you do? If you are lucky, you may have actually known the answer to one question. In addition, your guessing may have been more successful if you were able to use the process of elimination on any of the questions. Maybe you didn't know who the third Chief Justice was (question 3), but you knew that John Jay was the first. In that case, you would have eliminated choice **d** and therefore improved your odds of guessing right from one in four to one in three.

According to probability, you should get at least one question correct. If you answered two or three correctly, you may be a really terrific guesser. If you got none right, you may be a really bad guesser.

Keep in mind, though, that this is only a small sample. You should continue to keep track of your guessing ability as you work through the sample questions in this book. Circle the numbers of questions you guess on as you make your guess; or, if you don't have time during the practice tests, go back afterward, and try to remember at which questions you guessed the answers. Remember, on a test with four answer choices, your chance of getting a correct answer is one in four. So keep a separate guessing score for each exam. For example, how many questions did you guess? How many did you get right? If the number you got right is at least one-fourth of the number of questions you guessed on, you are at least an average guesser, maybe better—and you should always go ahead and guess on the real exam. If the number you got right is significantly lower than one-fourth of the number you guessed on, you would, frankly, be safe guessing anyway, but you might feel more comfortable if you guessed selectively, when you can eliminate a wrong answer or at least have a good feeling about one of the answer choices.

---

balanced diet. Be sure to eat plenty of fruits and vegetables, along with protein and carbohydrates. Foods that are high in lecithin (an amino acid), such as fish and beans, are especially good brain foods.

The night before the exam, you might eat plenty of carbohydrates, the way athletes do before a contest. Enjoy a big plate of spaghetti, rice and beans, or your own favorite carbohydrate.

Rest

You probably know how much sleep you need every night to be at your best, even if you don't always get it. Make sure you do get that much sleep, though, for at least a week before the exam. Moderation is important here, too. Extra sleep will just make you feel groggy.

If you are not a morning person and your exam will be given in the morning, you should reset your internal clock, so that your body doesn't think you are taking an exam at 3 A.M. You have to start this process

THE LEARNINGEXPRESS TEST PREPARATION SYSTEM

well before the exam: Get up half an hour earlier each morning, and then go to bed half an hour earlier that night. Don't try it the other way around; you will just toss and turn if you go to bed early without waking up early that same day. The next morning, get up another half an hour earlier, and so on. How long you will have to do this depends on how late you are used to waking up. Use the Physical Preparation Checklist below to help track your progress.

Physical Preparation Checklist

For the week before the exam, write down 1) what physical exercise you engaged in and for how long and 2) what you ate for each meal. Remember, you are trying for at least half an hour of exercise three days per week (preferably five days per week) and a balanced diet, which minimizes junk food intake.

7 days before the exam
Exercise: _____ for _____ minutes
Breakfast: _____
Lunch: _____
Dinner: _____
Snacks: _____

6 days before the exam
Exercise: _____ for _____ minutes
Breakfast: _____
Lunch: _____
Dinner: _____
Snacks: _____

5 days before the exam
Exercise: _____ for _____ minutes
Breakfast: _____
Lunch: _____
Dinner: _____
Snacks: _____

4 days before the exam
Exercise: _____ for _____ minutes
Breakfast: _____
Lunch: _____
Dinner: _____
Snacks: _____

3 days before the exam
Exercise: _____ for _____ minutes
Breakfast: _____
Lunch: _____
Dinner: _____
Snacks: _____

2 days before the exam
Exercise: _____ for _____ minutes
Breakfast: _____
Lunch: _____
Dinner: _____
Snacks: _____

1 day before the exam
Exercise: _____ for _____ minutes
Breakfast: _____
Lunch: _____
Dinner: _____
Snacks: _____

THE LEARNINGEXPRESS TEST PREPARATION SYSTEM

▶ Step 8: Make Final Test-Day Preparations

Time to complete: 10 minutes to read; time to complete will vary

Activity: Complete Final Preparations Checklist

If you remember some of the test-taking pitfalls from the beginning of this chapter, they included arriving late to the exam site and being cold as you complete the test. In this part of the LearningExpress Test Preparation System, you will learn how to take control over these external factors. Remember, you have already prepared your mind and body to take the exam, so now it's time to focus on these equally important details.

Final Preparations Checklist

Getting to the Exam Site

Location of exam site: _____

Date: _____

Departure time: _____

Do I know how to get to the exam site?   Yes ___   No ___

If no, make a trial run.

Time it will take to get to the exam site: _____

Things to lay out the night before

Clothes I will wear   _____

Sweater/jacket   _____

Watch   _____

Photo ID   _____

No. 2 pencils   _____

_____   _____

_____   _____

Find Out Where the Exam Is and Make a Trial Run

Do you know how to get to the exam site? Do you know how long it will take to get there? If not, make a trial run, preferably on the same day of the week at the same time of day. On the Final Preparations Checklist on page 24 make a note of the amount of time it will take you to get to the exam site. Plan on arriving at least 30–45 minutes early so you can orient yourself, use the bathroom, and calm down. Then calculate how early you need to wake up that morning, and make sure you awaken that early every day for a week before the exam. Remember, whether you are driving yourself or taking public transportation, you should leave ample time for any possible travel delays, including weather and traffic.

Gather Your Materials

The night before the exam, lay out your clothes and the materials you have to bring with you. Plan on dressing in layers; you won't have any control over the temperature of the examination room. Have a sweater or jacket you can take off if it's warm. Use the Final Preparations Checklist to help you gather everything you will need.

Don't Skip Breakfast

Even if you don't usually eat breakfast, do so on exam morning. A cup of coffee doesn't count. Don't do doughnuts or other sweet foods, either. A sugar high will leave you with a sugar low in the middle of the exam. A mix of protein and carbohydrates is best: Cereal (low sugar) with milk and just a little sugar, or eggs with toast, will give your body what it needs on test day.

▶ Step 9: Ace the Exam!

Time to complete: 10 minutes, plus test-taking time
Activity: Take the ASVAB and do your best!

Now that you have almost completed the LearningExpress Test Preparation System, you only have one more task. Imagine it is test day. You are ready. You made a study plan and followed through. You practiced your test-taking strategies while working through this book. You are in control of your physical, mental, and emotional state. You know when and where to show up and what to bring with you. In other words, you are better prepared than most of the other people taking the ASVAB with you.

When you are done with the exam, you will have earned a reward, so plan a celebration. Call up your friends and plan a party, or have a nice dinner for two—whatever your heart desires. Give yourself something to look forward to.

Go into the exam full of confidence, armed with the test-taking strategies you practiced until they became automatic. You are in control of yourself, your environment, and your performance on the exam. You are ready to succeed. So do it. Go in there and ace the exam. And look forward to your future in the military!

LESSON 3 ▶ Multiple-Choice Test Strategies

In this lesson, you will learn how to deal with the multiple-choice format and with questions requiring recall or recognition of material.

All multiple-choice test questions are geared toward testing your knowledge of a subject or toward measuring your skills at performing some task. Some test questions require you to recall specific items of information, while others ask you only to recognize information by separating it from similar choices. Others have you deduce answers based on ideas presented in the test itself.

Generally speaking, multiple-choice questions are considered to be objective questions because they are fact-based; they do not allow for the opinion or interpretation of the test taker. In addition, multiple-choice tests are easier and quicker to grade, and they do not penalize test takers who know the information but have poorly developed writing skills or problems with expressive language.

MULTIPLE-CHOICE TEST STRATEGIES

▶ Parts of a Multiple-Choice Question

You may remember taking tests that contained questions like this one:

1. The largest of the Great Lakes is
   a. Huron.
   b. Superior.
   c. Erie.
   d. Mississippi.

The question contains the three elements of most multiple-choice questions, which are stems, options, and distracters.

> **Stem:** "The largest of the Great Lakes is"
> **Options:** All answer choices
> **Distracters:** Incorrect answer choices

The answer is **b**.

Stems

Stems contain the core information on which the question is based. In some tests, the stems of the questions may be as long as a paragraph and could contain a lot of information that you must sift through before you can choose an answer. Sometimes stem questions are phrased as situations. Situation questions set a scene or provide facts from which you base your answers to a series of questions.

Stems can also be simply a word, a math example, or a fragment of a sentence that serves to frame the question.

Options

Options are the answer choices offered to you. Many options require that you simply recognize a correct choice among several others.

2. As president, Ronald Reagan came to be known as
   a. Old Hickory.
   b. The Great Communicator.
   c. Speaker of the House.
   d. Old Ironsides.

The answer is **b**.

In the next sample, the question is trying to test the accuracy of your knowledge by offering two or more options that are similar.

3. The word in the following sentence that means the same or almost the same as *flammable* is
   a. fireproof.
   b. fire resistant.
   c. easily burned.
   d. burning.

To answer this question, it wouldn't be enough to know that flammable has something to do with fire. All of the options offer that choice. You have to know that the meaning of flammable is *easily burned*, answer **c**.

Distracters

Distracters are the incorrect answers, which often present a challenge to you. In question 2, the distracters are **a**, **c**, and **d**; and in question 3, they are **a**, **b**, and **d**.

Distracters are often written to force you to be very careful in your selections. In question 2, for instance, if you didn't know that Reagan was known as The Great Communicator, you could be distracted by the two choices that refer to age. Since Reagan was one of our oldest presidents while in office, you might be tempted to choose one of them.

The wise test taker will eliminate the clearly impossible options first. In question 2, both Old Ironsides, which is the name of a ship, and Speaker of the House, which is an office that cannot be held by a sitting president, should be eliminated. Then, between Old Hickory and The Great Communicator, you would have to make a choice. If you remembered that Old Hickory was the term used to describe President Andrew Jackson, you would eliminate it, and then the correct choice would be obvious.

▶ Recognition and Recall Questions

As noted before, multiple-choice questions require you to recall or recognize specific information that is surrounded by other similar, but incorrect, options. These other options are written in such a way that they confuse many test takers.

4. Choose the word or phrase that means the same or almost the same as the word *secession*.
    a. a meeting
    b. the act of breaking away from a political body
    c. a surgical birth
    d. a parade

5. From the following group, circle the word that is correctly spelled.
    a. chanel
    b. channel
    c. chanle
    d. chanell

6. Choose the correct word for the following sentence: I went to _____ house for lunch.
    a. they're
    b. their
    c. there
    d. the're

In questions 4–6, you would have to rely on your memory for the definition of secession, the spelling of the word *channel*, and the correct word *their*, or you would have to be able to recognize the correct answer in comparison to the other choices. The correct answers are: 4 is **b**, 5 is **b**, and 6 is **b**.

Note distracters **c** and **d** in question 4. Many multiple-choice questions are designed to confuse you by offering options that sound like the stem word or have associations with the stem word. In this instance, the similarity between *procession* and *secession*, and the distant but confusing sound similarities between *secession* and the medical shorthand *C-section* (for cesarean section) could trap the unwary test taker.

▶ Reading Questions

Some multiple-choice questions are geared toward measuring your ability to take information directly from the text and to answer questions based on that text. These kinds of multiple-choice questions typically measure reading comprehension—you will see them mostly in the Paragraph Comprehension subtest.

Generally, reading comprehension tests start with a passage on a particular subject, followed by as few as two or as many as ten questions based on the content of that passage.

These questions usually are aimed at four skills:

1. recognizing the definition of a vocabulary word in the passage
2. identifying the main idea of the passage
3. noting a specific fact or detail in the passage
4. making an inference or conclusion based on information in the passage that is not directly stated

MULTIPLE-CHOICE TEST STRATEGIES

Read the following passage and the four questions that follow. Identify each type of question from the previous list.

The "broken window" theory was originally developed to explain how minor acts of vandalism or disrespect can quickly escalate to crimes and attitudes that break down the entire social fabric of an area or unit. It is an idea that can easily be applied to any situation in society. The theory contends that if a broken window in an abandoned building is not replaced quickly, soon all the windows in that building will be broken.

In other words, a small violation, if condoned, leads others to commit similar or greater violations. Thus, after all the windows have been broken, the building is likely to be further vandalized. According to this theory, violations increase exponentially. Thus, if disrespect to a superior is tolerated, others will be tempted to be disrespectful as well. A management crisis could erupt literally overnight.

For example, if one firefighter begins to disregard proper housewatch procedure by neglecting to maintain the housewatch administrative journal, and this firefighter is not reprimanded, others will follow suit by committing similar violations of procedure, thinking, "If he can get away with it, why can't I?" So what starts out as a small violation that may not seem to warrant disciplinary action, may actually ruin the efficiency of the entire firehouse, risking the lives of the people the firehouse serves.

7. In this passage, the word *reprimanded* means
   a. scolded.
   b. praised.
   c. rewarded.
   d. fired.
Question type_____

8. The best title for this passage would be
   a. Broken Windows: Only the First Step.
   b. The Importance of Housewatch.
   c. How to Write an Administrative Journal.
   d. A Guide to Window Repair.
Question type_____

9. The passage suggests that
   a. firefighters are sloppy administrators.
   b. firefighters will blame others for mistakes.
   c. discipline starts with small infractions.
   d. discipline is important for the efficiency of the firehouse.
Question type_____

10. According to the passage, which of the following could be the result of broken windows?
   a. The building would soon be vandalized.
   b. Firefighters would lose morale.
   c. There could be a management crisis.
   d. The efficiency of the firehouse could be destroyed.
Question type_____

Answers
   7. a. Reprimanded means scolded. (Vocabulary)
   8. a. The passage is about the "broken window" theory, showing that a minor violation or breach of discipline can lead to major violations. (Main idea)
   9. d. The passage applies the broken window theory to firehouse discipline, showing that even small infractions have to be dealt with to avoid worse problems later. (Inference)
   10. a. See the third sentence of the passage. (Detail)

MULTIPLE-CHOICE TEST STRATEGIES

▶ Strategies for Answer Reading Questions

A successful test taker will approach multiple-choice questions with several good strategies. They include:

1. **Always circle or underline the key words in the question.** Key words in the stem often direct you to the correct answer.
2. **Immediately eliminate all clearly incorrect distracters.** This will usually mean that you have to choose between two similar choices.
3. **Carefully read each question.** Beware of look-alike options, easily confused options, and silly options. Watch for tricky wording such as, All of the following are true EXCEPT . . .
4. **Understand exactly what is being asked.** You will find distracters that are accurate and may sound right but do not apply to the question.
5. **Beware of the absolute.** Read carefully for words like *always*, *never*, *none*, or *all*. An answer may sound perfectly correct and the general principal may be correct, however, it may not be true in all circumstances. For example, think about the statement "All roses are red." *All* roses?
6. **Do the easiest questions first.** Many tests are arranged so that the questions move from easy to more difficult. Don't lose points by skipping those early questions and risk running out of time.

▶ Math Questions

Math questions on the ASVAB assess how you apply basic math skills to workplace situations.

Some questions are mostly numerical in format:

1. What is the reciprocal of $3\frac{7}{8}$?
   a. $\frac{31}{28}$
   b. $\frac{8}{31}$
   c. $\frac{8}{21}$
   d. $\frac{31}{8}$

Some questions are introduced by stems in which the numerical information is embedded. In other words, they are word problems.

2. A city worker is paid time-and-a-half per hour in overtime pay. He earns $20 per hour. If he works four hours more than his contracted work week, how much does he make in overtime pay?
   a. 80.00
   b. 120.00
   c. 400.00
   d. 60.00

Answers
1. b. $3\frac{7}{8} = \frac{31}{8}$, whose reciprocal is $\frac{8}{31}$.
2. b. The worker makes $20 \times 1\frac{1}{2} = \$30$ per hour in overtime. Now multiply the hourly overtime wage by the number of overtime hours: $30 \times 4 = 120$.

Strategies for Answering Math Questions

Even though you are dealing with numbers and not words in math questions, the way you analyze the questions and consider the possible answers is very similar.

- **Don't panic because it's math.** They're only numbers after all.
- **Read the stem carefully.** Underline or circle the most important information in the stem.
- **Read all the options carefully.** Don't be confused by distracting answer choices.
- **Work through the problem.** If you immediately see an answer that matches, you can move right on. Do all calculations on paper, not in your head.

- **Skip unfamiliar or difficult questions on the first pass through the test.** Put a dot in the margin of the test or circle the questions so that you can locate the question quickly and easily if you are in a hurry.
- **Be careful when you write your calculations.** The number 1 can look like 7, 3 like 8, and 6 like 0 when you are in a hurry. If you don't take your time and write carefully, you risk choosing a wrong answer or wasting time recalculating an answer to find something that fits from your choice of answers.
- **Translate numbers from math into English.** *Reciprocal* in question 1 means the inverse of the fractional number. Time and a half in question 2 means $1\frac{1}{2}$ or $\frac{3}{2}$. Take some time to translate words from English into math.

▶ Managing Your Time

It's important to manage your time so that you don't get stuck on any one question. The following section will help you pace yourself so that you increase your chances for getting all the points you can get in the time you are allowed.

Read or Listen to Directions Carefully

If you are allowed, always underline or circle key words in the instructions that cue you to what the question requires. Follow the directions to the letter.

Preview the Test

There should be no surprises when you get to any section of the test. It's always helpful to know what you will encounter on the test.

There are two reasons that you should preview a test carefully before you start working:

- You want to locate weak spots on the test, so that you can prepare to spend more time on those sections.
- You want to be familiar with the content and format of the whole test so that you have a good overall picture of what topics are stressed and how questions are presented.

Don't Linger Too Long on Any One Question

Answer the questions that you know the answers to for certain right away. If you are unsure about a question, put a dot in the margin next to that question so that you can find it easily when you want to come back to it later. Don't linger too long over questions you can't answer right away.

When You Have Time Left Over

If you have followed the strategies and conscientiously maintained control over your timing, you may find that you have time left over after finishing the test. Do not throw down your pen and sigh with relief that the test is over—at least not yet. Remember, this is not a race. You don't win by being first over the finish line. Here are some suggestions for making the best possible use of any time left over:

- **Don't leave anything out.** Make sure that you did not skip any questions and that you have answers for any questions you may have left blank the first time through the test. Use the tips you learned about guessing to help you answer questions about which you are still uncertain.
- **Double-check your answers.** Make sure each answer you have chosen is entered on the correct spot on the answer sheet. If you change an answer, make sure you change it completely.

The strategies in this lesson should help you prepare for, take, and excel on the ASVAB. The rest of the lessons in this book will help improve your skills for the Arithmetic Reasoning, Mathematics Knowledge, Paragraph Comprehension, and Word Knowledge portions of the ASVAB.

SECTION 2

Math for the Arithmetic Reasoning and Mathematics Knowledge Subtests

The Arithmetic Reasoning and Mathematics Knowledge subtests of the ASVAB cover math skills. Arithmetic Reasoning is mostly composed of math word problems. Mathematics Knowledge tests knowledge of math concepts, principles, and procedures. You don't have to do a lot of calculation in the Mathematics Knowledge subtest; you need to know basic terminology (like *sum* and *perimeter*), formulas (such as the area of a square), and computation rules. Both subtests cover the subjects you might have studied in school. This section of the book reviews concepts you will need for both Arithmetic Reasoning and Mathematics Knowledge.

▶ Math Strategies

- **Don't work in your head!** Use your test book or scratch paper to take notes, draw pictures, and calculate. Although you might think that you can solve math questions more quickly in your head, that's a good way to make mistakes. Write out each step.
- **Read a math question in chunks rather than straight through from beginning to end.** As you read each chunk, stop to think about what it means and make notes or draw a picture to represent that chunk.
- **When you get to the actual question, circle it.** This will keep you more focused as you solve the problem.
- **Glance at the answer choices for clues.** If they are fractions, you probably should do your work in fractions; if they are decimals, you should probably work in decimals; etc.

MATH FOR THE ARITHMETIC REASONING AND MATHEMATICS KNOWLEDGE SUBTESTS

- **Make a plan of attack to help you solve the problem.**
- **If a question stumps you, try one of the *backdoor* approaches explained in the next section.** These are particularly useful for solving word problems.
- **When you get your answer, reread the circled question to make sure you have answered it.** This helps avoid the careless mistake of answering the wrong question.
- **Check your work after you get an answer.** Test takers get a false sense of security when they get an answer that matches one of the multiple-choice answers. Here are some good ways to check your work *if you have time:*
  - Ask yourself if your answer is reasonable, if it makes sense.
  - Plug your answer back into the problem to make sure the problem holds together.
  - Do the question a second time, but use a different method.
- **Approximate when appropriate.** For example:
  - $5.98 + $8.97 is a little less than $15. (Add: $6 + $9)
  - .9876 × 5.0342 is close to 5. (Multiply: 1 × 5)
- **Skip hard questions and return to them later.** Mark them in your test book so you can find them quickly.

Backdoor Approaches for Answering Tough Questions

Many word problems are actually easier to solve by backdoor approaches. The two techniques that follow are time-saving ways to solve perplexing multiple-choice word problems with a straightforward approach. The first technique, *nice numbers*, is useful when there are unknowns (like x) in the text of the word problem, making the problem too abstract for you. The second technique, *working backward*, presents a quick way to substitute numeric answer choices back into the problem to see which one works.

Nice Numbers

1. When a question contains unknowns, like x, plug in nice numbers for the unknowns. A nice number is easy to calculate with and makes sense in the problem.
2. Read the question with the nice numbers in place. Then solve it.
3. If the answer choices are all numbers, the choice that matches your answer is the right one.
4. If the answer choices contain unknowns, substitute the same nice numbers into all the answer choices. The choice that matches your answer is the right one. If more than one answer matches, do the problem again with different nice numbers. You will only have to check the answer choices that have already matched.

Example:

Judi went shopping with p dollars in her pocket. If the price of shirts was s shirts for d dollars, what is the maximum number of shirts Judi could buy with the money in her pocket?

a. psd
b. $\frac{ps}{d}$
c. $\frac{pd}{s}$
d. $\frac{ds}{p}$

To solve this problem, let's try these nice numbers: $p = $100, s = 2; d = 25. Now reread it with the numbers in place:

Judi went shopping with $100 in her pocket. If the price of shirts was 2 shirts for $25, what is the maximum number of shirts Judi could buy with the money in her pocket?

Since 2 shirts cost $25, that means that 4 shirts cost $50, and 8 shirts cost $100. So our answer is 8. Let's substitute the nice numbers into all 4 answers:

MATH FOR THE ARITHMETIC REASONING AND MATHEMATICS KNOWLEDGE SUBTESTS

    a. $100 \times 2 \times 25 = 5{,}000$
    b. $\frac{100 \times 2}{25} = 8$
    c. $\frac{100 \times 25}{2} = 1{,}250$
    d. $\frac{25 \times 2}{100} = \frac{1}{2}$

The answer is **b** because it is the only one that matches our answer of 8.

Working Backward

You can frequently solve a word problem by plugging the answer choices back into the text of the problem to see which one fits all the facts stated in the problem. The process is faster than you think because you will probably only have to substitute one or two answers to find the right one.

    This approach works only when:

- All of the answer choices are numbers.
- You are asked to find a simple number, not a sum, product, difference, or ratio.

Here's What to Do

1. Look at all the answer choices and begin with the one in the middle of the range. For example, if the answers are 14, 8, 2, 20, and 25, begin by plugging 14 into the problem.
2. If your choice doesn't work, eliminate it. Determine if you need a bigger or smaller answer.
3. Plug in one of the remaining choices.
4. If none of the answers work, you may have made a careless error. Begin again or look for your mistake.

Example:

Juan ate $\frac{1}{3}$ of the jellybeans. Maria then ate $\frac{3}{4}$ of the remaining jellybeans, which left 10 jellybeans. How many jellybeans were there to begin with?
    a. 60
    b. 80
    c. 90
    d. 120

Starting with the middle answer, let's assume there were 90 jellybeans to begin with:

    Since Juan ate $\frac{1}{3}$ of them, that means he ate 30 ($\frac{1}{3} \times 90 = 30$), leaving 60 of them ($90 - 30 = 60$). Maria then ate $\frac{3}{4}$ of the 60 jellybeans, or 45 of them ($\frac{3}{4} \times 60 = 45$). That leaves 15 jellybeans ($60 - 45 = 15$).

The problem states that there were 10 jellybeans left, and we wound up with 15 of them. That indicates that we started with too big a number. Thus, 90 and 120 are incorrect! With only two choices left, let's use common sense to decide which one to try. The next lower answer is only a little smaller than 90 and may not be small enough. So, let's try 60:

    Since Juan ate $\frac{1}{3}$ of them, that means he ate 20 ($\frac{1}{3} \times 60 = 20$), leaving 40 of them ($60 - 20 = 40$). Maria then ate $\frac{3}{4}$ of the 40 jellybeans, or 30 of them ($\frac{3}{4} \times 40 = 30$). That leaves 10 jellybeans ($40 - 30 = 10$).

Because this result of 10 jellybeans remaining agrees with the problem, the correct answer is **a**.

Glossary of Terms

Denominator   the bottom number in a fraction. *Example:* 2 is the denominator in $\frac{1}{2}$.

Difference   subtract. The difference of two numbers means subtract one number from the other.

Divisible by   a number is divisible by a second number if that second number divides *evenly* into the original number. *Example:* 10 is divisible by 5 (10 ÷ 5 = 2, with no remainder). However, 10 is not divisible by 3. (See *multiple of*)

Even Integer   integers that are divisible by 2, like . . . –4, –2, 0, 2, 4. . . (See *integer*)

Integer   numbers along the number line, like . . . –3, –2, –1, 0, 1, 2, 3. . . Integers include the whole numbers and their opposites. (See *whole number*)

Multiple of   a number is a multiple of a second number if that second number can be multiplied by an integer to get the original number. *Example:* 10 is a multiple of 5 (10 = 5 × 2); however, 10 is not a multiple of 3. (See *divisible by*)

Negative Number   a number that is less than zero, like . . . –1, –18.6, $-\frac{3}{4}$. . .

Numerator   the top part of a fraction. *Example:* 1 is the numerator of $\frac{1}{2}$.

Odd Integer   integers that are not divisible by 2, like . . . –5, –3, –1, 1, 3. . .

Positive Number   a number that is greater than zero, like . . . 2, 42, $\frac{1}{2}$, 4.63. . .

Prime Number   integers that are divisible only by 1 and themselves, like . . . 2, 3, 5, 7, 11. . . All prime numbers are odd, except for the number 2. The number 1 is not considered prime.

Product   multiply. The product of two numbers means the numbers are multiplied together.

Quotient   the answer you get when you divide. *Example:* 10 divided by 5 is 2; the quotient is 2.

Real Number   all the numbers you can think of, like . . . 17, –5, $\frac{1}{2}$, –23.6, 3.4329, 0. . . Real numbers include the integers, fractions, and decimals. (See *integer*)

Remainder   the number left over after division. *Example:* 11 divided by 2 is 5, with a remainder of 1.

Sum   add. The sum of two numbers means the numbers are added together.

Whole Number   numbers you can count on your fingers, like . . . 1, 2, 3. . . All whole numbers are positive.

L E S S O N

  Basic Arithmetic Functions

▶ Adding Whole Numbers

When we add numbers, we are combining two or more groups to find the total. The total is often called the **sum**.

For example, suppose you have 5 cans of soup in your kitchen cupboard, and you buy 4 more. Now you have a total of 9 cans of soup. The number 9 is the sum (total), of the two groups.

Now, suppose you want to add two or more larger groups. To add larger numbers correctly, follow these simple rules:

1. Line up the numbers in a straight column. Arrange the numbers according to place value.
2. Add each column. Start the addition at the right with the ones column.
3. Make sure your answers are in the correct columns.

Example: At the store where you buy your soup, there are 132 cans on the shelves. The stocker adds 56 more cans. You want to know how many cans there are in all. The problem, written out, would look like this: 132 + 56.

BASIC ARITHMETIC FUNCTIONS

To find the answer, follow the three steps:

1. Line up the numbers in a straight column.
   132 = 1 hundred 3 tens 2 ones
   +56 =   5 tens 6 ones

2. Add each column. Start the addition at the right with the ones column:
   1 hundred 3 tens 2 ones
   +   5 tens 6 ones
   1   8   8

3. Make sure your answers are in the correct columns:
   132 = 1 hundred 3 tens 2 ones
   +56 =   5 tens 6 ones
   188 = 1 hundred 8 tens 8 ones

Copy the numbers into columns and add.

_____ **1.** 567 + 12

_____ **2.** 3,004 + 1,790

_____ **3.** 24 + 831

_____ **4.** 22 + 513 + 104

_____ **5.** 1,526 + 40

_____ **6.** 10,412 + 30 + 1,547

Carrying

When you add a column of numbers, the sum may be 10 or more. For example, if your ones column adds up to 14, you have a total of 1 ten and 4 ones. Now you must carry the 1 to the tens column.

To carry, follow these simple rules:

1. Line up the numbers to be added in a straight column.
2. Add the numbers in the ones place.
3. If the sum is 10 or more, write the number in the tens place at the top of the next column.
4. Add the tens column, starting with the number you carried.
5. Add the other columns in the same way.

Example: 238 + 76

1. Line up the numbers to be added in a straight column:
   238
   +76

2. Add the numbers in the ones place:
   6
   +8
   14

3. If the sum is 10 or more, carry the number in the tens place to the top of the next column:
   1
   238
   +76
     4

4. Add the tens column, starting with the number you carried:
   1
   3
   +7
   11

5. Add the other columns in the same way:
   1 1
   238
   +76
   314

Copy the numbers into columns and add.

_____ **7.** 499 + 78

_____ **8.** 16 + 9 + 27

BASIC ARITHMETIC FUNCTIONS

_____ **9.** 1,465 + 2,808

_____ **10.** 367 + 20,553

_____ **11.** 351 + 42 + 86 + 5

_____ **12.** 19 + 1,600 + 782 + 62

▶ Subtracting

When you subtract two numbers, you are finding the difference between them.

Here are some questions answered by subtraction:

- When we take 4 away from 9, how many are left?
- What is the difference between 4 and 9?
- What is 9 minus 4?
- How much more is 9 than 4?
- To get 9, how much must be added to 4?

To subtract, follow these simple rules:

1. Line up the numbers in a column. Arrange the numbers according to place value.
2. Start the subtraction at the right with the ones column.
3. Make sure your answers are in the correct columns.

Example: 98 − 75

1. Line up the numbers in a column. Arrange the numbers according to place value:
   98 =   9 tens and 8 ones
   −75 = −7 tens and 5 ones

2. Start the subtraction at the right with the ones column:
   9 tens and 8 ones
   −7 tens and 5 ones
      2   3

3. Make sure your answers are in the correct columns:
   98 =   9 tens and 8 ones
   −75 = −7 tens and 5 ones
   23   2 tens and 3 ones

Copy the numbers into columns and subtract.

_____ **13.** 48 − 17

_____ **14.** 79 − 39

_____ **15.** 156 − 44

_____ **16.** 992 − 61

_____ **17.** 3,667 − 2,005

_____ **18.** 235 − 112

Borrowing

Sometimes the top number in a column is larger than the bottom number. Then you must borrow from the next column. Borrowing is also known as **regrouping**.

To borrow, follow these simple rules:

1. Line up the columns by place value, as usual.
2. Start with the right column, the ones place. If you cannot subtract the bottom number from the top number, borrow from the tens place. Write the new numbers at the top of each column.
3. Continue subtracting from right to left.
4. Optional: Check the result by adding.

Example: 52 − 36

1. Line up the columns by place value, as usual:
   52 =   5 tens and 2 ones
   −36 = − 3 tens and 6 ones

2. Start with the right column, the ones place. If you cannot subtract the bottom number from the top number, borrow from the tens place. (Since you cannot subtract 6 from 2, you must borrow from the 5 in the tens place.) Write the new numbers at the top of each column:

$$\begin{array}{r} 4\ 12 = 4\text{ tens and} 12\text{ ones} \\ \cancel{52} = \cancel{5\text{ tens and 2 ones}} \\ -36 = -3\text{ tens and 6 ones} \end{array}$$

Notice that you are taking 1 ten (10 ones) and adding it to the ones place. Now you have 12 ones: $2 + 10 = 12$. You have also taken one ten away from the tens place: $5 - 1 = 4$.

3. Continue subtracting from right to left:

$$\begin{array}{r} 4\ 12 \\ \cancel{52} \\ -36 \\ \hline 16 \end{array}$$

4. Optional: Check the result by adding: $16 + 36 = 52$.

Practice.

_____ **19.** $37 - 28$

_____ **20.** $61 - 14$

_____ **21.** $193 - 88$

_____ **22.** $465 - 277$

_____ **23.** $1{,}381 - 497$

_____ **24.** $22{,}623 - 13{,}884$

▶ Multiplying Whole Numbers

Multiplication is the short method of adding a number to itself several times. (The sign for multiplication is ×.) For example, 4×2, read 4 times 2 means $2 + 2 + 2 + 2$. If you add 4 twos together, you will get a total of 8. So $4 \times 2 = 8$. In multiplication, the two numbers multiplied are called **factors**. The result of multiplying one number by another is called the **product**. This means that 8 is the product of 4 times 2.

We use multiplication to put together equal groups. Suppose you had 3 packs of gum. Each pack has 5 sticks. You have 3 groups of 5. You want to find out how many sticks of gum you have total. You could add $5 + 5 + 5$. But a shorter way is multiply 3 times 5.

$3 \times 5 = 15$

Sometimes it is helpful to view equal groups in rows or columns. If you add all the blocks in the figure below, you will get a total of 24. A shorter way is to multiply. There are 6 blocks in the rows across. There are 4 blocks in the up-and-down rows.

$4 \times 6 = 24$

BASIC ARITHMETIC FUNCTIONS

Multiplication Table

It is important that you commit to memory all the multiplication facts up to 12. Use the multiplication table to help you. The second row across will give you the result of all the numbers multiplied by 1 (1 × 1 = 1; 1 × 2 = 2; 1 × 3 = 3; and so forth). The next row will give you the result of all the numbers multiplied by 2 (2 × 1 = 2; 2 × 2 = 4). Memorize the multiplication table before you read the preceding math chapters.

	1	2	3	4	5	6	7	8	9	10	11	12
1	1	2	3	4	5	6	7	8	9	10	11	12
2	2	4	6	8	10	12	14	16	18	20	22	24
3	3	6	9	12	15	18	21	24	27	30	33	36
4	4	8	12	16	20	24	28	32	36	40	44	48
5	5	10	15	20	25	30	35	40	45	50	55	60
6	6	12	18	24	30	36	42	48	54	60	66	72
7	7	14	21	28	35	42	49	56	63	70	77	84
8	8	16	24	32	40	48	56	64	72	80	88	96
9	9	18	27	36	45	54	63	72	81	90	99	108
10	10	20	30	40	50	60	70	80	90	100	110	120
11	11	22	33	44	55	66	77	88	99	110	121	132
12	12	24	36	48	60	72	84	96	108	120	132	144

Here are a few more tips to help you learn multiplication.

- You may have already noticed that the order of the numbers (factors) doesn't change the result: 7 × 2 = 14 and 2 × 7 = 14. In other words, 7 groups of 2 equals 2 groups of 7.
- In multiplication, when one of the factors is zero, the product is zero: 7 × 0 = 0 and 0 × 7 = 0. This is true no matter how large the number: 1 × 0 = 0 and 1,000,000 × 0 = 0.

Multiplying by One-Digit Numbers

To multiply whole numbers:

1. Line up the numbers by place value.
2. Begin multiplying in the ones place. If necessary, carry to the next column.
3. Continue multiplying from right to left. Add any numbers that were carried.

BASIC ARITHMETIC FUNCTIONS

Example: 6 × 27

1. Line up the numbers by place value:
    27
    × 6

2. Begin multiplying in the ones place. If necessary carry to the next column. (6 × 7 = 42. Carry 4 tens to the tens place.)
    4
    27
    × 6
    2

3. Continue multiplying from right to left. Add any numbers that were carried.
    (6 × 2 = 12 and 12 + 4 = 16):
    4
    27
    × 6
    162

Multiply.

_____ **25.** 63 × 2

_____ **26.** 79 × 7

_____ **27.** 48 × 3

_____ **28.** 109 × 8

_____ **29.** 530 × 6

_____ **30.** 800 × 9

Multiplying by Numbers with Two or More Digits

The following will help you learn to multiply with two (or more) digit numbers. There are three steps.

1. Multiply as usual by the number in the ones place.
2. Multiply by the number in the tens place. (For larger numbers continue to line up the numbers according to place value.) Write this product (result) in the tens place under the first product.
3. Add the columns.

Example: 34 × 26

1. Multiply as usual by the number in the ones place: (6 × 34 = 204)
    2
    34
    × 26
    204

2. Multiply by the number in the tens place. Write this product (result) in the tens place under the first product. If you want, you can put a zero in the ones place as a place holder. (2 × 34 = 68):
    34
    × 26
    204
    680

Note that the 8 is aligned with the 2 in the multiplier and that the zero serves as a place holder so that you align the numbers correctly. (To multiply with three [or more] digit numbers, multiply the third product in the hundreds place.)

3. Add the columns:
    34
    × 26
    204
    + 680
    884

42

BASIC ARITHMETIC FUNCTIONS

Multiply.

_____ **31.** 77 × 11

_____ **32.** 98 × 32

_____ **33.** 85 × 45

_____ **34.** 456 × 53

_____ **35.** 612 × 22

_____ **36.** 128 × 141

▶ Dividing Whole Numbers

Division means dividing an amount into equal groups. Suppose you have 12 cookies. You want to divide them equally among 3 people. You want 3 groups out of a total of 12. To do this, you need to use division.

$$12 \div 3 = 4$$

When you divide 12 equally into 3 groups, you have 4 in each group. The sign ÷ means *divided by*.

Division Is the Opposite of Multiplication

You learned earlier that subtraction is the opposite of addition. Division is the opposite of multiplication:

$$12 \div 3 = 4 \text{ and } 4 \times 3 = 12$$

You need practice to learn basic division facts. Memorize them as you did multiplication. You can use the multiplication table as a guide. Read it in reverse.

The Language of Division

The quantity to be divided is called the **dividend**. The number of equal parts is called the **divisor**. The result is called the **quotient**.

$$40 \text{ (dividend)} \div 5 \text{ (divisor)} = 8 \text{ (quotient)}$$

Another way to write out this problem would be:

$$5 \overline{)40}^{\,8}$$

One more way to write this problem would be: $\frac{40}{5} = 8$

More to Remember about Division

When you divide any number by itself, the result is 1: $8 \div 8 = 1$

When you divide any number by 1, the result is the number itself: $8 \div 1 = 8$

When zero is divided by another number, the result is zero: $0 \div 8 = 0$

Dividing by One-Digit Numbers

There are several steps to division. In these steps, you will use addition, subtraction, and multiplication.

Here are the steps to division:

1. Write the problem correctly.
2. Estimate and divide.
3. Write your answer on top.
4. Multiply and write your answer below.
5. Subtract.
6. Bring down.
7. Repeat the steps if necessary.

Example: 216 ÷ 9

1. Write the problem correctly:
   $9 \overline{)216}$

BASIC ARITHMETIC FUNCTIONS

2. Estimate and divide: You cannot divide 9 into 2. So you must divide 9 into 21. Think about how many times 9 will go into 21. Nine times 3 = 27 is too large, so try 2.

3. Write your answer on top:

    $$\begin{array}{r} 2 \\ 9\overline{)216} \end{array}$$

Notice that your answer is written above the tens place. (If you are able to divide evenly into the hundreds place, the answer is written above the hundreds place.)

4. Multiply (9 × 2 = 18) and write your answer below:

    $$\begin{array}{r} 2 \\ 9\overline{)216} \\ 18 \end{array}$$

5. Subtract (21 − 18 = 3):

    $$\begin{array}{r} 2 \\ 9\overline{)216} \\ -18 \\ \hline 3 \end{array}$$

6. Bring down (6):

    $$\begin{array}{r} 2 \\ 9\overline{)216} \\ -18 \\ \hline 36 \end{array}$$

7. Repeat the steps if necessary (36 ÷ 9 = 4):

    $$\begin{array}{r} 24 \\ 9\overline{)216} \\ -18 \\ \hline 36 \\ -36 \\ \hline 0 \end{array}$$

Remainders

Sometimes the quotient (answer) will not be exact. You will have a number left over. This number is called a **remainder**. This means that you have a certain number of equal groups with one or more left over. Let's say you have 13 cookies instead of 12. You want to divide them into 3 groups. You will still have 3 groups of 4. But now you will have one cookie remaining. You can show that there is a remainder by writing an R and the number left over beside the answer. 13 ÷ 3 = 4 R1

Checking Your Work

To check your work in division:

1. Multiply your answer (the quotient) by the divisor.
2. Add any remainder. Is your answer the dividend (the number you divided into)? Then your work is correct.

Divide.

_____ **37.** 65 ÷ 5

_____ **38.** 256 ÷ 4

_____ **39.** 37 ÷ 6

_____ **40.** 188 ÷ 3

_____ **41.** 5,511 ÷ 4

_____ **42.** 2,929 ÷ 9

Dividing by Two- or Three-Digit Numbers

The steps for dividing by two- or three-digit numbers are the same. However, you are dividing by a larger number in the first step.

BASIC ARITHMETIC FUNCTIONS

Divide.

_____ **43.** 325 ÷ 25

_____ **44.** 381 ÷ 127

_____ **45.** 1,941 ÷ 96

_____ **46.** 4,207 ÷ 18

_____ **47.** 40,000 ÷ 20

_____ **48.** 11,000 ÷ 550

▶ **Answers**

1. 579
2. 4,794
3. 855
4. 639
5. 1,566
6. 11,989
7. 577
8. 52
9. 4,273
10. 20,920
11. 484
12. 2,463
13. 31
14. 40
15. 112
16. 931

17. 1,662
18. 123
19. 9
20. 47
21. 105
22. 188
23. 884
24. 8,739
25. 126
26. 553
27. 144
28. 872
29. 3,180
30. 7,200
31. 847
32. 3,136
33. 3,825
34. 24,168
35. 13,464
36. 18,048
37. 13
38. 64
39. 6 R1
40. 62 R2
41. 1,377 R3
42. 325 R4
43. 13
44. 3
45. 20 R21
46. 233 R13
47. 2,000
48. 20

LESSON 5

Fractions, Decimals, Percents, and Averages

▶ Fractions

Problems involving fractions may be straightforward calculation questions, or they may be word problems. Typically, they ask you to add, subtract, multiply, divide, or compare fractions.

Working with Fractions
A fraction is a part of something.

Example: Let's say that a pizza was cut into eight equal slices and you ate three of them. The fraction $\frac{3}{8}$ tells you what part of the pizza you ate. The pizza below shows this: Three of the eight pieces (the pieces you ate) are shaded.

FRACTIONS, DECIMALS, PERCENTS, AND AVERAGES

THREE KINDS OF FRACTIONS	
Proper fraction	The top number is less than the bottom number: $\frac{1}{2}; \frac{2}{3}; \frac{4}{9}; \frac{8}{13}$ The value of a proper fraction is less than 1.
Improper fraction	The top number is greater than or equal to the bottom number: $\frac{3}{2}; \frac{5}{3}; \frac{14}{9}; \frac{12}{12}$ The value of an improper fraction is 1 or more.
Mixed number	A fraction written to the right of a whole number: $3\frac{1}{2}; 4\frac{2}{3}; 12\frac{3}{4}; 24\frac{3}{4}$ The value of a mixed number is more than 1: It is the sum of the whole number plus the fraction.

Changing Improper Fractions into Mixed or Whole Numbers

It's easier to add and subtract fractions that are mixed numbers rather than improper fractions. To change an improper fraction, say $\frac{13}{2}$, into a mixed number, follow these steps:

1. Divide the bottom number (2) into the top number (13) to get the whole number portion (6) of the mixed number:

$$\begin{array}{r} 6 \\ 2\overline{)13} \\ \underline{12} \\ 1 \end{array}$$

2. Write the remainder of the division (1) over the old bottom number (2): $6\frac{1}{2}$
3. Check: Change the mixed number back into an improper fraction (see steps below).

Changing Mixed Numbers into Improper Fractions

It's easier to multiply and divide fractions when you're working with improper fractions rather than mixed numbers. To change a mixed number, say $2\frac{3}{4}$, into an improper fraction, follow these steps:

1. Multiply the whole number (2) by the bottom number (4): $2 \times 4 = 8$
2. Add the result (8) to the top number (3): $8 + 3 = 11$
3. Put the total (11) over the bottom number (4): $\frac{11}{4}$
4. Check: Reverse the process by changing the improper fraction into a mixed number. If you get back the number you started with, your answer is correct.

Reducing Fractions

Reducing a fraction means writing it in *lowest terms*, that is, with smaller numbers. For instance, 50¢ is $\frac{50}{100}$ of a dollar, or $\frac{1}{2}$ of a dollar. In fact, if you have 50¢ in your pocket, you could say that you have half a dollar. Reducing a fraction does not change its value.

FRACTIONS, DECIMALS, PERCENTS, AND AVERAGES

Follow these steps to reduce a fraction:

1. Find a whole number that divides *evenly* into both numbers that make up the fraction.
2. Divide that number into the top of the fraction, and replace the top of the fraction with the quotient (the answer you got when you divided).
3. Do the same thing to the bottom number.
4. Repeat the first three steps until you can't find a number that divides evenly into both numbers of the fraction.

For example, let's reduce $\frac{8}{24}$. We could do it in two steps: $\frac{8 \div 4}{24 \div 4} = \frac{2}{6}$; then $\frac{2 \div 2}{6 \div 2} = \frac{1}{3}$. Or we could do it in a single step: $\frac{8 \div 8}{24 \div 8} = \frac{1}{3}$.

Shortcut: When the top and bottom numbers both end in zeroes, cross out the same number of zeroes in both numbers to begin the reducing process. For example $\frac{300}{4,000}$ reduces to $\frac{3}{40}$ when you cross out two zeroes in both numbers.

Whenever you do arithmetic with fractions, reduce your answer. On a multiple-choice test, don't panic if your answer isn't listed. Try to reduce it and then compare it to the choices.

Reduce these fractions to lowest terms.

1. $\frac{3}{12} =$

2. $\frac{14}{35} =$

3. $\frac{27}{72} =$

Raising Fractions to Higher Terms

Before you can add and subtract fractions, you have to know how to raise a fraction to higher terms. This is actually the opposite of reducing a fraction.

Follow these steps to raise $\frac{2}{3}$ to 24ths:

1. Divide the old bottom number (3) into the new one (24): $\quad\quad\quad\quad \frac{3}{24} = 8$
2. Multiply the answer (8) by the old top number (2): $\quad\quad\quad\quad\quad 2 \times 8 = 16$
3. Put the answer (16) over the new bottom number (24): $\quad\quad\quad\quad \frac{16}{24}$
4. Check: Reduce the new fraction to see if you get back the original one: $\frac{16 \div 8}{24 \div 8} = \frac{2}{3}$

Raise these fractions to higher terms.

4. $\frac{5}{12} = \frac{}{24}$

5. $\frac{2}{9} = \frac{}{27}$

6. $\frac{2}{5} = \frac{}{500}$

Adding Fractions

If the fractions have the same bottom numbers, just add the top numbers together and write the total over the bottom number.

Examples: $\frac{2}{9} + \frac{4}{9} = \frac{6}{9}$ Reduce the sum: $\frac{2}{3}$.

$\frac{5}{8} + \frac{7}{8} = \frac{12}{8}$ Change the sum to a mixed number: $1\frac{4}{8}$; then reduce: $1\frac{1}{2}$.

There are a few extra steps to add mixed numbers with the same bottom numbers, say $2\frac{3}{5} + 1\frac{4}{5}$:

1. Add the fractions: $\frac{3}{5} + \frac{4}{5} = \frac{7}{5}$
2. Change the improper fraction into a mixed number: $\frac{7}{5} = 1\frac{2}{5}$
3. Add the whole numbers: $2 + 1 = 3$
4. Add the results of steps 2 and 3: $1\frac{2}{5} + 3 = 4\frac{2}{5}$

Finding the Least Common Denominator

If the fractions you want to add don't have the same bottom number, you will have to raise some or all of the fractions to higher terms so that they all have the same bottom number, called the **common denominator**. All of the original bottom numbers divide evenly into the common denominator. If it is the smallest number that they all divide evenly into, it is called the **least common denominator (LCD)**.

Here are a few tips for finding the LCD, the smallest number that all the bottom numbers evenly divide into:

- See if all the bottom numbers divide evenly into the biggest bottom number.
- Look at a multiplication table of the largest bottom number until you find a number that all the other bottom numbers evenly divide into.
- When all else fails, multiply all the bottom numbers together.

Example: $\frac{2}{3} + \frac{4}{5}$

1. Find the LCD. Multiply the bottom numbers: $3 \times 5 = 15$
2. Raise each fraction to 15ths: $\frac{2}{3} = \frac{10}{15}$
   $+ \frac{4}{5} = \frac{12}{15}$
3. Add as usual: $\frac{22}{15}$

FRACTIONS, DECIMALS, PERCENTS, AND AVERAGES

Try these addition problems.

7. $\frac{3}{4} + \frac{1}{6} =$

8. $\frac{7}{8} + \frac{2}{3} + \frac{3}{4} =$

9. $4\frac{1}{3} + 2\frac{3}{4} + \frac{1}{6} =$

Subtracting Fractions

If the fractions have the same bottom numbers, just subtract the top numbers and write the difference over the bottom number.

Example: $\frac{4}{9} - \frac{3}{9} = \frac{4-3}{9} = \frac{1}{9}$

If the fractions you want to subtract don't have the same bottom number, you will have to raise some or all of the fractions to higher terms, so that they all have the same bottom number, or LCD. If you forgot how to find the LCD, just read the section on adding fractions with different bottom numbers.

Example: $\frac{5}{6} - \frac{3}{4}$

1. Raise each fraction to 12ths because 12 is the LCD, the smallest number that 6 and 4 both divide into evenly:
2. Subtract as usual:

$$\frac{5}{6} = \frac{10}{12}$$
$$-\frac{3}{4} = \frac{9}{12}$$
$$\frac{1}{12}$$

Subtracting mixed numbers with the same bottom number is similar to adding mixed numbers.

Example: $4\frac{3}{5} - 1\frac{2}{5}$

1. Subtract the fractions: $\quad \frac{3}{5} - \frac{2}{5} = \frac{1}{5}$
2. Subtract the whole numbers: $\quad 4 - 1 = 3$
3. Add the results of steps 1 and 2: $\quad \frac{1}{5} + 3 = 3\frac{1}{5}$

Sometimes there is an extra step where you borrow when subtracting mixed numbers with the same bottom numbers, say $7\frac{3}{5} - 2\frac{4}{5}$:

1. You can't subtract the fractions the way they are because $\frac{4}{5}$ is bigger than $\frac{3}{5}$. So you borrow 1 from the 7, making it 6, and change that 1 to $\frac{5}{5}$ because 5 is the bottom number: $\quad 7\frac{3}{5} = 6\frac{5}{5} + \frac{3}{5}$
2. Add the numbers from Step 1: $\quad 6\frac{5}{5} + \frac{3}{5} = 6\frac{8}{5}$
3. Now you have a different version of the original problem: $\quad 6\frac{8}{5} - 2\frac{4}{5}$
4. Subtract the fractional parts of the two mixed numbers: $\quad \frac{8}{5} - \frac{4}{5} = \frac{4}{5}$
5. Subtract the whole number parts of the two mixed numbers: $\quad 6 - 2 = 4$
6. Add the results of the last two steps together: $\quad 4 + \frac{4}{5} = 4\frac{4}{5}$

FRACTIONS, DECIMALS, PERCENTS, AND AVERAGES

Try these subtraction problems.

10. $\frac{4}{5} - \frac{2}{3} =$

11. $\frac{7}{8} - \frac{1}{4} - \frac{1}{2} =$

12. $4\frac{1}{3} - 2\frac{3}{4} =$

Now let's put what you have learned about adding and subtracting fractions to work in some real-life problems.

13. Manuel drove $3\frac{1}{2}$ miles to work. Then he drove $4\frac{3}{4}$ miles to the store. When he left there, he drove 2 miles to the dry cleaners. Then he drove $3\frac{2}{3}$ miles back to work for a meeting. Finally, he drove $3\frac{1}{2}$ miles home. How many miles did he travel in total?

   a. $17\frac{5}{12}$
   b. $16\frac{5}{12}$
   c. $15\frac{7}{12}$
   d. $15\frac{5}{12}$

14. Before leaving the warehouse, a truck driver noted that the mileage gauge registered $4,357\frac{4}{10}$ miles. When he arrived at the delivery location, the mileage gauge then registered $4,400\frac{1}{10}$ miles. How many miles did he drive from the warehouse to the delivery location?

   a. $42\frac{3}{10}$
   b. $42\frac{7}{10}$
   c. $43\frac{7}{10}$
   d. $47\frac{2}{10}$

Multiplying Fractions

Multiplying fractions is actually easier than adding them. All you do is multiply the top numbers and then multiply the bottom numbers.

Examples: $\frac{2}{3} \times \frac{5}{7} = \frac{2 \times 5}{3 \times 7} = \frac{10}{21}$

$\frac{1}{2} \times \frac{3}{5} \times \frac{7}{4} = \frac{1 \times 3 \times 7}{2 \times 5 \times 4} = \frac{21}{40}$

Sometimes you can *cancel* before multiplying. Canceling is a shortcut that makes the multiplication go faster because you're multiplying with smaller numbers. It's very similar to reducing: If there is a number that divides evenly into a top number and bottom number, do that division before multiplying. If you forget to cancel, you will still get the right answer, but you will have to reduce it.

FRACTIONS, DECIMALS, PERCENTS, AND AVERAGES

Example: $\frac{5}{6} \times \frac{9}{20}$

1. Cancel the 6 and the 9 by dividing 3 into both of them: 6 ÷ 3 = 2 and 9 ÷ 3 = 3. Cross out the 6 and the 9.
2. Cancel the 5 and the 20 by dividing 5 into both of them: 5 ÷ 5 = 1 and 20 ÷ 5 = 4. Cross out the 5 and the 20.
3. Multiply across the new top numbers and the new bottom numbers: $\frac{1 \times 3}{2 \times 4} = \frac{3}{8}$.

Try these multiplication problems.

15. $\frac{1}{5} \times \frac{2}{3} =$

16. $\frac{2}{3} \times \frac{4}{7} \times \frac{3}{5} =$

17. $\frac{3}{4} \times \frac{8}{9} =$

To multiply a fraction by a whole number, first rewrite the whole number as a fraction with a bottom number of 1.

Example: $5 \times \frac{2}{3} = \frac{5}{1} \times \frac{2}{3} = \frac{10}{3}$
(Optional: Convert $\frac{10}{3}$ to a mixed number: $3\frac{1}{3}$)

To multiply with mixed numbers, it's easier to change them to improper fractions before multiplying.

Example: $4\frac{2}{3} \times 5\frac{1}{2}$

1. Convert $4\frac{2}{3}$ to an improper fraction: $\qquad 4\frac{2}{3} = \frac{(4 \times 3 + 2)}{3} = \frac{14}{3}$

2. Convert $5\frac{1}{2}$ to an improper fraction: $\qquad 5\frac{1}{2} = \frac{(5 \times 2 + 1)}{2} = \frac{11}{2}$

3. Cancel and multiply the fractions: $\qquad \frac{\cancel{14}^{7}}{3} \times \frac{11}{\cancel{2}_{1}} = \frac{77}{3}$

4. Optional: Convert the improper fraction to a mixed number: $\qquad \frac{77}{3} = 25\frac{2}{3}$

Now try these multiplication problems with mixed numbers and whole numbers.

18. $4\frac{1}{3} \times \frac{2}{5} =$

19. $2\frac{1}{2} \times 6 =$

20. $3\frac{3}{4} \times 4\frac{2}{5} =$

FRACTIONS, DECIMALS, PERCENTS, AND AVERAGES

Here are a few more real-life problems to test your skills.

21. After driving $\frac{2}{3}$ of the 15 miles to work, Mr. Stone stopped to make a phone call. How many miles had he driven when he made his call?
   a. 5
   b. $7\frac{1}{2}$
   c. 10
   d. 12

22. If Henry worked $\frac{3}{4}$ of a 40-hour week, how many hours did he work?
   a. $7\frac{1}{2}$
   b. 10
   c. 25
   d. 30

23. Technician Chin makes $14.00 an hour. When she works more than 8 hours a day, she gets overtime pay of $1\frac{1}{2}$ times her regular hourly wage for the extra hours. How much did she earn for working 11 hours in one day?
   a. $77
   b. $154
   c. $175
   d. $210

Dividing Fractions

To divide one fraction by a second fraction, invert the second fraction (that is, flip the top and bottom numbers) and then multiply.

   Example: $\frac{1}{2} \div \frac{3}{5}$

1. Invert the second fraction ($\frac{3}{5}$): $\frac{5}{3}$
2. Change the division sign (÷) to a multiplication sign (×).
3. Multiply the first fraction by the new second fraction: $\frac{1}{2} \times \frac{5}{3} = \frac{1 \times 5}{2 \times 3} = \frac{5}{6}$

To divide a fraction by a whole number, first change the whole number to a fraction by putting it over 1. Then follow the division steps above.

   Example: $\frac{3}{5} \div 2 = \frac{3}{5} \div \frac{2}{1} = \frac{3}{5} \times \frac{1}{2} = \frac{3 \times 1}{5 \times 2} = \frac{3}{10}$

When the division problem has a mixed number, convert it to an improper fraction, and then divide as usual.

FRACTIONS, DECIMALS, PERCENTS, AND AVERAGES

Example: $2\frac{3}{4} \div \frac{1}{6}$

1. Convert $2\frac{3}{4}$ to an improper fraction: $\quad 2\frac{3}{4} = \frac{2 \times 4 + 3}{4} = \frac{11}{4}$

2. Divide $\frac{11}{4}$ by $\frac{1}{6}$: $\quad \frac{11}{4} \div \frac{1}{6} = \frac{11}{4} \times \frac{6}{1}$

3. Flip $\frac{1}{6}$ to $\frac{6}{1}$ change ÷ to ×, cancel and multiply: $\quad \frac{11}{4} \times \frac{6}{1} = \frac{11 \times 3}{2 \times 1} = \frac{33}{2}$

Here are a few division problems to try.

24. $\frac{1}{3} \div \frac{2}{3} =$

25. $2\frac{3}{4} \div \frac{1}{2} =$

26. $\frac{3}{5} \div 3 =$

27. $3\frac{3}{4} \div 2\frac{1}{3} =$

Let's wrap this up with some real-life problems.

28. If four friends evenly split $6\frac{1}{2}$ pounds of candy, how many pounds of candy does each friend get?
   a. $\frac{8}{13}$
   b. $1\frac{5}{8}$
   c. $1\frac{1}{2}$
   d. $1\frac{5}{13}$

29. How many $2\frac{1}{2}$-pound chunks of cheese can be cut from a single 20-pound piece of cheese?
   a. 2
   b. 4
   c. 6
   d. 8

30. Ms. Goldbaum earned $36.75 for working $3\frac{1}{2}$ hours. What was her hourly wage?
   a. $10.00
   b. $10.50
   c. $10.75
   d. $12.00

FRACTIONS, DECIMALS, PERCENTS, AND AVERAGES

▶ Decimals

A decimal is a special kind of fraction. You use decimals every day when you deal with money—$10.35 is a decimal that represents 10 dollars and 35 cents. The decimal point separates the dollars from the cents. Because there are 100 cents in one dollar, 1¢ is $\frac{1}{100}$ of a dollar, or $.01.

Each decimal digit to the right of the decimal point has a name:

Examples: $.1 = 1$ tenth $= \frac{1}{10}$
$.02 = 2$ hundredths $= \frac{2}{100}$
$.003 = 3$ thousandths $= \frac{3}{1,000}$
$.0004 = 4$ ten-thousandths $= \frac{4}{10,000}$

When you add zeros after the rightmost decimal place, you don't change the value of the decimal. For example, 6.17 is the same as all of these:

6.170
6.1700
6.17000000000000000

If there are digits on both sides of the decimal point (like 10.35), the number is called a **mixed decimal**. If there are digits only to the right of the decimal point (like .53), the number is called a **decimal**. A whole number (like 15) is understood to have a decimal point at its right (15.). Thus, 15 is the same as 15.0, 15.00, 15.000, and so on.

Changing Fractions to Decimals

To change a fraction to a decimal, divide the bottom number into the top number after you put a decimal point and a few zeros on the right of the top number. When you divide, bring the decimal point up into your answer.

Example: Change $\frac{3}{4}$ to a decimal.

1. Add a decimal point and two zeros to the top number (3):   3.00
2. Divide the bottom number (4) into 3.00:
   Bring the decimal point up into the answer:

   $$\begin{array}{r} .75 \\ 4\overline{)3.00} \\ \underline{2\ 8} \\ 20 \\ \underline{20} \\ 0 \end{array}$$

3. The quotient (result of the division) is the answer: .75

Some fractions may require you to add many decimal zeros in order for the division to come out evenly. In fact, when you convert a fraction like $\frac{2}{3}$ to a decimal, you can keep adding decimal zeros to the top number forever because the division will never come out evenly. As you divide 3 into 2, the number 6 will keep repeating:

$$2 \div 3 = .6666666666 \text{ etc.}$$

This is called a **repeating decimal** and it can be written as $.6\overline{66}$ or as $.66\frac{2}{3}$. You can approximate it as .67, .667, .6667, and so on.

FRACTIONS, DECIMALS, PERCENTS, AND AVERAGES

Changing Decimals to Fractions

To change a decimal to a fraction, write the digits of the decimal as the top number of a fraction and write the decimal's name as the bottom number of the fraction. Then reduce the fraction, if possible.

Example: .018

1. Write 18 as the top of the fraction: $\quad\quad\quad\quad\quad\quad\quad\quad\quad\quad \frac{18}{}$
2. Three places to the right of the decimal means *thousandths*, so write 1,000 as the bottom number: $\quad\quad\quad\quad\quad\quad \frac{18}{1,000}$
3. Reduce by dividing 2 into the top and bottom numbers: $\quad \frac{18 \div 2}{1,000 \div 2} = \frac{9}{500}$

Change these decimals or mixed decimals to fractions.

31. .005 =

32. 3.48 =

33. 123.456 =

Comparing Decimals

Because decimals are easier to compare when they have the same number of digits after the decimal point, tack zeros onto the end of the shorter decimals. Then all you have to do is compare the numbers as if the decimal points weren't there:

Example: Compare .08 and .1.

1. Tack one zero at the end of .1: .10
2. To compare .10 to .08, just compare 10 to 8.
3. Since 10 is larger than 8, .1 is larger than .08.

Adding and Subtracting Decimals

To add or subtract decimals, line them up so their decimal points are aligned. You may want to tack on zeros at the end of shorter decimals so you can keep all your digits lined up evenly. Remember, if a number doesn't have a decimal point, then put one at the right end of the number.

Example: 1.23 + 57 + .038 =

1. Line up the numbers like this:
2. Add.

```
   1.230
  57.000
 + .038
  58.268
```

Example: 1.23 − .038 =

1. Line up the numbers like this:
2. Subtract.

```
  1.230
 − .038
  1.192
```

FRACTIONS, DECIMALS, PERCENTS, AND AVERAGES

Try these addition and subtraction problems.

34. .905 + .02 + 3.075 =

35. .005 + 8 + .3 =

36. 3.48 − 2.573 =

37. 123.456 − 122 =

38. A park ranger drove 3.7 miles to the state park. He then walked 1.6 miles around the park to make sure everything was all right. He got back into the car, drove 2.75 miles to check on a broken light and then drove 2 miles back to the ranger station. How many miles did he drive in total?
   a. 8.05
   b. 8.45
   c. 10
   d. 10.05

39. The average number of customers at a diner fell from 486.4 per week to 402.5 per week. By how many customers per week did the average fall?
   a. 73.9
   b. 83
   c. 83.1
   d. 83.9

Multiplying Decimals

To multiply decimals, ignore the decimal points and just multiply the numbers. Then count the total number of decimal digits (the digits to the *right* of the decimal point) in the numbers you are multiplying. Count off that number of digits in your answer beginning at the right side and put the decimal point to the *left* of those digits.

Example: 215.7 × 2.4

1. Multiply 2157 times 24:

$$\begin{array}{r} 2157 \\ \times 24 \\ \hline 8628 \\ 4314 \\ \hline 51768 \end{array}$$

FRACTIONS, DECIMALS, PERCENTS, AND AVERAGES

2. Because there is a total of two decimal digits in 215.7 and 2.4, count off two places from the right in 51768, placing the decimal point to the *left* of the last two digits: 517.68

If your answer doesn't have enough digits, tack zeros on to the left of the answer.

Example: .03 × .006

1. Multiply 3 times 6: $\qquad$ 3 × 6 = 18
2. You need five decimal digits in your answer, so tack on three zeros: $\qquad$ 00018
3. Put the decimal point at the front of the number (which is five digits in from the right): $\qquad$ .00018

You can practice multiplying decimals with these.

40. .05 × .6 =

41. .053 × 6.4 =

42. 38.1 × .0184 =

43. Joe earns $14.50 per hour. Last week, he worked 37.5 hours. How much money did he earn that week?
   a. $518.00
   b. $518.50
   c. $536.50
   d. $543.75

44. Nuts cost $3.50 per pound. Approximately how much will 4.25 pounds of nuts cost?
   a. $12.25
   b. $12.88
   c. $14.50
   d. $14.88

FRACTIONS, DECIMALS, PERCENTS, AND AVERAGES

Dividing Decimals

To divide a decimal by a whole number, set up the division, $8\overline{).256}$, and immediately bring the decimal point straight up into the answer, $8\overline{).256}$. Then divide as you would normally divide whole numbers.

Example:
$$\begin{array}{r} .032 \\ 8\overline{).256} \\ \underline{0} \\ 25 \\ \underline{24} \\ 16 \\ \underline{16} \\ 0 \end{array}$$

There is an extra step to perform before you can divide any number by a decimal. Move the decimal point to the very right of the number you are dividing by, counting the number of places you are moving it. Then move the decimal point the same number of places to the right in the number you are dividing into. In other words, first change the problem to one in which you are dividing by a whole number.

Example: $.06\overline{)1.218}$

1. Because there are two decimal digits in .06, move the decimal point two places to the right in both numbers and move the decimal point straight up into the answer:

   $.06.\overline{)1.21.8}$

2. Divide using the new numbers:

$$\begin{array}{r} 20.3 \\ 6\overline{)121.8} \\ \underline{12} \\ 01 \\ \underline{00} \\ 18 \\ \underline{18} \\ 0 \end{array}$$

Under certain conditions, you have to tack on zeros to the right of the last decimal digit in the number you are dividing into:

- if there are not enough digits for you to move the decimal point to the right.
- if the answer doesn't come out evenly when you do the division.
- if you are dividing a whole number by a decimal. Then you will have to tack on the decimal point as well as some zeros.

FRACTIONS, DECIMALS, PERCENTS, AND AVERAGES

Try your skills on these division problems.

45. $7\overline{)9.8} =$

46. $.0004\overline{).0512} =$

47. $.5\overline{)28.6} =$

48. $.14\overline{)196} =$

49. If James Worthington drove his truck 92.4 miles in 2.1 hours, what was his average speed in miles per hour?
   a. 41
   b. 44
   c. 90.3
   d. 94.5

50. Mary Sanders walked a total of 18.6 miles in 4 days. On average, how many miles did she walk each day?
   a. 4.15
   b. 4.60
   c. 4.65
   d. 22.60

▶ Percents

A percent is a special kind of fraction or part of something. The bottom number (the **denominator**) is always 100. For example, 17% is the same as $\frac{17}{100}$. Literally, the word *percent* means *per 100 parts*. The root *cent* means 100: A *century* is 100 years; there are 100 *cents* in a dollar, etc. Thus, 17% means 17 parts out of 100. Because fractions can also be expressed as decimals, 17% is also equivalent to .17, which is 17 hundredths.

You come into contact with percents every day. Sales tax, interest, and discounts are just a few common examples.

If your fraction skills need work, you may want to review that section again before reading further.

Changing a Decimal to a Percent and Vice Versa

To change a decimal to a percent, move the decimal point two places to the right and tack on a percent sign (%) at the end. If the decimal point moves to the very right of the number, you don't have to write the decimal point. If there aren't enough places to move the decimal point, add zeros on the right before moving the decimal point.

To change a percent to a decimal, drop off the percent sign and move the decimal point two places to the left. If there aren't enough places to move the decimal point, add zeros on the left before moving the decimal point.

FRACTIONS, DECIMALS, PERCENTS, AND AVERAGES

Try changing these decimals to percents.

51. .45 =

52. .008 =

53. .16$\frac{2}{3}$ =

Now, change these percents to decimals.

54. 12% =

55. 87$\frac{1}{2}$% =

56. 250% =

Changing a Fraction to a Percent and Vice Versa

To change a fraction to a percent, there are two techniques. Each is illustrated by changing the fraction $\frac{1}{4}$ to a percent:

Technique 1:   Multiply the fraction by 100%.
  Multiply $\frac{1}{4}$ by 100%: $\frac{1}{4} \times \frac{\overset{25}{\cancel{100}}\%}{1} = 25\%$.

Technique 2:   Divide the fraction's bottom number into the top number; then move the decimal point two places to the right and tack on a percent sign (%).
  Divide 4 into 1 and move the decimal point two places to the right:

$$4\overline{)1.00}^{\;.25} \qquad\qquad .25 = 25\%$$

To change a percent to a fraction, remove the percent sign and write the number over 100. Then reduce if possible.

Example: Change 4% to a fraction.

1. Remove the % and write the fraction 4 over 100: $\frac{4}{100}$
2. Reduce: $\frac{4 \div 4}{100 \div 4} = \frac{1}{25}$

Here's a more complicated example: Change 16$\frac{2}{3}$% to a fraction.

1. Remove the % and write the fraction 16$\frac{2}{3}$ over 100: $\frac{16\frac{2}{3}}{100}$
2. Since a fraction means "top number divided by bottom number," rewrite the fraction as a division problem: $16\frac{2}{3} \div 100$
3. Change the mixed number (16$\frac{2}{3}$) to an improper fraction ($\frac{50}{3}$): $\frac{50}{3} \div \frac{100}{1}$
4. Flip the second fraction ($\frac{100}{1}$) and multiply: $\frac{\cancel{50}^{1}}{3} \times \frac{1}{\cancel{100}_{2}} = \frac{1}{6}$

FRACTIONS, DECIMALS, PERCENTS, AND AVERAGES

Try changing these fractions to percents.

57. $\frac{1}{8} =$

58. $\frac{13}{25} =$

59. $\frac{7}{12} =$

Now change these percents to fractions.

60. 95% =

61. $37\frac{1}{2}\% =$

62. 125% =

Sometimes it is more convenient to work with a percentage as a fraction or a decimal. Rather than always *calculating* the equivalent fraction or decimal, consider memorizing the equivalence table below. Not only will this increase your efficiency on the math test, but it will also be practical for real-life situations.

CONVERSION TABLE		
DECIMAL	**%**	**FRACTION**
.25	25%	$\frac{1}{4}$
.50	50%	$\frac{1}{2}$
.75	75%	$\frac{3}{4}$
.10	10%	$\frac{1}{10}$
.20	20%	$\frac{1}{5}$
.40	40%	$\frac{2}{5}$
.60	60%	$\frac{3}{5}$
.80	80%	$\frac{4}{5}$
$.33\overline{3}$	$33\frac{1}{3}\%$	$\frac{1}{3}$
$.66\overline{6}$	$66\frac{2}{3}\%$	$\frac{2}{3}$

FRACTIONS, DECIMALS, PERCENTS, AND AVERAGES

Percent Word Problems

Word problems involving percents come in three main varieties:

- Find a percent of a whole.
    Example: What is 30% of 40?
- Find what percent one number is of another number.
    Example: 12 is what percent of 40?
- Find the whole when the percent of it is given.
    Example: 12 is 30% of what number?

While each variety has its own approach, there is a single shortcut formula you can use to solve each of these:

$$\frac{is}{of} = \frac{\%}{100}$$

The *is* is the number that usually follows or is just before the word *is* in the question.
The *of* is the number that usually follows the word *of* in the question.
The % is the number that is in front of the % or *percent* in the question.

Or you may think of the shortcut formula as:

$$\frac{part}{whole} = \frac{\%}{100}$$

$$part \times 100 = whole \times \%$$

To solve each of the three varieties, let's use the fact that the **cross-products** are equal. The cross-products are the products of the numbers diagonally across from each other. Remembering that *product* means *multiply*, here's how to create the cross-products for the percent shortcut:

$$\frac{part}{whole} = \frac{\%}{100}$$

$$part \times 100 = whole \times \%$$

Here's how to use the shortcut with cross-products:

- Find a percent of a whole.
    What is 30% of 40?
    30 is the % and 40 is the *of* number: $\frac{is}{40} = \frac{30}{100}$
    Cross-multiply and solve for *is*: $is \times 100 = 40 \times 30$
    $is \times 100 = 1{,}200$
    $12 \times 100 = 1{,}200$

    Thus, **12 is** 30% of 40.

64

FRACTIONS, DECIMALS, PERCENTS, AND AVERAGES

- Find what percent one number is of another number.
    12 is what percent of 40?
    12 is the *is* number and 40 is the *of* number: $\frac{12}{40} = \frac{\%}{100}$
    Cross-multiply and solve for %: $12 \times 100 = 40 \times \%$
    $1{,}200 = 40 \times \%$
    $1{,}200 = 40 \times \mathbf{30}$

    Thus, 12 is **30% of** 40.

- Find the whole when the percent of it is given.
    12 is 30% of what number?
    12 is the *is* number and 30 is the %: $\frac{12}{of} = \frac{30}{100}$
    Cross-multiply and solve for the *of* number: $12 \times 100 = of \times 30$
    $1{,}200 = of \times 30$
    $1{,}200 = \mathbf{40} \times 30$

    Thus 12 is 30% **of 40**.

You can use the same technique to find the percent increase or decrease. The *is* number is the actual increase or decrease, and the *of* number is the original amount.

   Example: If a merchant puts his $20 hats on sale for $15, by what percent does he decrease the selling price?

1. Calculate the decrease, the *is* number: $20 - $15 = $5
2. The *of* number is the original amount, $20.
3. Set up the equation and solve for *of* by cross-multiplying: $\frac{5}{20} = \frac{\%}{100}$
    $5 \times 100 = 20 \times \%$
    $500 = 20 \times \%$
    $500 = 20 \times 25$

4. Thus, the selling price is decreased by **25%**.
    If the merchant later raises the price of the hats from $15 $\frac{5}{15} = \frac{\%}{100}$
    back to $20, don't be fooled into thinking that the percent $5 \times 100 = 15 \times \%$
    increase is also 25%! It's actually more, because the $500 = 15 \times \%$
    increase amount of $5 is now based on a lower original
    price of only $15: $500 = 15 \times 33\frac{1}{3}$
    Thus, the selling price is increased by **33%**.

FRACTIONS, DECIMALS, PERCENTS, AND AVERAGES

Find a percent of a whole.

63. 1% of 25 =

64. 18.2% of 50 =

65. $37\frac{1}{2}$% of 100 =

66. 125% of 60 =

Find what percent one number is of another number.

67. 10 is what % of 20?

68. 4 is what % of 12?

69. 12 is what % of 4?

Find the whole when the percent of it is given.

70. 15% of what number is 15?

71. $37\frac{1}{2}$% of what number is 3?

72. 200% of what number is 20?

Now try your percent skills on some real-life problems.

73. Last Monday, 20% of 140 staff members were absent. How many employees were absent that day?
   a. 14
   b. 28
   c. 112
   d. 126

74. Forty percent of Vero's postal service employees are women. If there are 80 women in Vero's postal service, how many men are employed there?
   a. 32
   b. 112
   c. 120
   d. 160

FRACTIONS, DECIMALS, PERCENTS, AND AVERAGES

75. Of the 840 shirts sold at a retail store last month, 42 had short sleeves. What percent of the shirts were short sleeved?
   a. .5%
   b. 2%
   c. 5%
   d. 20%

76. Sam's Shoe Store put all of its merchandise on sale for 20% off. If Jason saved $10 by purchasing one pair of shoes during the sale, what was the original price of the shoes before the sale?
   a. $12
   b. $20
   c. $40
   d. $50

▶ Averages

An average, also called an **arithmetic mean**, is a number that *typifies* a group of numbers, a measure of central tendency. You come into contact with averages on a regular basis: your bowling average, the average grade on a test, the average number of hours you work per week.

To calculate an average, add up the number of items being averaged and divide by the number of items.

Example: What is the average of 6, 10, and 20?
Solution: Add the three numbers together and divide by 3: $\frac{6 + 10 + 20}{3} = 12$

Shortcut
Here's a neat shortcut for some average problems.

- Look at the numbers being averaged. If they are equally spaced, like 5, 10, 15, 20, and 25, then the average is the number in the middle, or 15 in this case.
- If there is an even number of such numbers, say 10, 20, 30, and 40, then there is no middle number. In this case, the average is halfway between the two middle numbers. In this case, the average is halfway between 20 and 30, or 25.
- If the numbers are almost evenly spaced, you can probably estimate the average without going to the trouble of actually computing it. For example, the average of 10, 20, and 32 is just a little more than 20, which is the middle number.

FRACTIONS, DECIMALS, PERCENTS, AND AVERAGES

Try these average questions.

77. Bob's bowling scores for the last five games were 180, 182, 184, 186, and 188. What was his average bowling score?
   a. 182
   b. 183
   c. 184
   d. 185

78. Conroy averaged 30 miles an hour for the two hours he drove in town and 60 miles an hour for the two hours he drove on the highway. What was his average speed in miles per hour?
   a. 18
   b. $22\frac{1}{2}$
   c. 45
   d. 60

79. There are 10 females and 20 males in a history class. If the females achieved an average score of 85 and the males achieved an average score of 95, what was the class average? (Hint: Don't fall for the trap of taking the average of 85 and 95; there are more scores of 95 being averaged than 85.)
   a. $90\frac{2}{3}$
   b. $91\frac{2}{3}$
   c. 92
   d. $92\frac{2}{3}$

▶ Answers

Fractions

1. $\frac{1}{4}$
2. $\frac{2}{5}$
3. $\frac{3}{8}$
4. 10
5. 6
6. 200
7. $\frac{11}{12}$
8. $\frac{55}{24}$ or $2\frac{7}{24}$
9. $7\frac{1}{4}$
10. $\frac{2}{15}$
11. $\frac{1}{8}$
12. $\frac{19}{12}$ or $1\frac{7}{12}$
13. a.
14. b.
15. $\frac{2}{15}$
16. $\frac{8}{35}$
17. $\frac{2}{3}$
18. $\frac{26}{15}$ or $1\frac{11}{15}$
19. 15
20. $\frac{33}{2}$ or $16\frac{1}{2}$
21. c.

FRACTIONS, DECIMALS, PERCENTS, AND AVERAGES

22. d.
23. c.
24. $\frac{1}{2}$
25. $5\frac{1}{2}$
26. $\frac{1}{5}$
27. $\frac{45}{28}$ or $1\frac{17}{28}$
28. b.
29. d.
30. b.

Decimals

31. $\frac{5}{1,000}$ or $\frac{1}{200}$
32. $3\frac{12}{25}$
33. $123\frac{456}{1,000}$ or $123\frac{57}{125}$
34. 4
35. 8.305
36. 0.907
37. 1.456
38. b.
39. d.
40. 0.03
41. 0.3392
42. 0.70104
43. d.
44. d.
45. 1.4
46. 128
47. 57.2
48. 1,400
49. b.
50. c.

Percents

51. 45%
52. 0.8%
53. 16.67% or $16\frac{2}{3}$%
54. 0.12
55. 0.875
56. 2.5
57. 12.5% or $12\frac{1}{2}$%
58. 52%
59. 58.33% or $58\frac{1}{3}$%
60. $\frac{19}{20}$
61. $\frac{3}{8}$
62. $\frac{5}{4}$ or $1\frac{1}{4}$
63. $\frac{1}{4}$ or .25
64. 9.1
65. $37\frac{1}{2}$ or 37.5
66. 75
67. 50%
68. $33\frac{1}{3}$%
69. 300%
70. 100
71. 8
72. 10
73. b.
74. c.
75. c.
76. d.

Averages

77. c.
78. c.
79. b.

LESSON

Geometry and Algebra

▶ Geometry

Typically, there are very few geometry problems on the math sections. The problems that are included tend to cover the basics: lines, angles, triangles, rectangles, squares, and circles. You may be asked to find the area or perimeter of a particular shape or the size of an angle. The arithmetic involved is pretty simple, so all you really need are a few definitions and formulas.

Glossary of Geometry Terms

Angle two rays with a common endpoint called a vertex. There are four types of angles:
  Acute: less than 90°
  Obtuse: more than 90°
  Right: 90°
  Straight: 180°

Circle set of all points that are the same distance from the center.
  Area = πr^2
  Circumference = $2\pi r$
  (π = 3.14; r = radius)

Circumference distance around a circle. (See *circle*)

Diameter a line through the center of a circle. The diameter is twice the length of the radius. (See *circle*, *radius*)

Line extends endlessly in both directions. It is referred to by a letter at the end of it or by two points on it. Thus, the line below may be referred to as line *l* or as $\overleftrightarrow{AB}$.

Parallel lines two lines in the same plane that do not intersect.
  l || *m*

Perimeter distance around a figure, such as a triangle or a rectangle. The perimeter of a circle is called its *circumference*.
  Perimeter = sum of length of all sides

Perpendicular lines two lines in the same plane that intersect to form four right angles. (See *right angle*)

Point has a location but no size or dimension. It is referred to by a letter close to it, like this: • A

Radius line segment from the center to any point on a circle. The radius is half the diameter. (See *circle*, *diameter*)

Glossary of Geometry Terms (continued)

Rectangle   four-sided figure with a right angle and both pairs of opposite sides parallel (which implies that all four sides are right angles and that opposite sides are equal in length).
Area = length × width
Perimeter = 2 × length + 2 × width

Square   rectangle with four equal sides (See *rectangle*).
Area = (side)²
Perimeter = 4 × side

Triangle   three-sided figure.
Area = ½(base × height)
Perimeter = sum of the lengths of all three sides
Angles: The sum of the three angles of a triangle is always 180°.

Practice Problems in Geometry
Try these sample problems.

1. What is the area in inches of a triangle with base 10" and height 8"?
   a. 80
   b. 40
   c. 20
   d. 10

2. Find the perimeter of a triangle with sides of length 3, 4, and 5 units.
   a. 60 units
   b. 20 units
   c. 12 units
   d. 9 units

3. If the area of a square field measures 256 square feet, how many feet of fencing are needed to completely surround the field?
   a. 256
   b. 128
   c. 64
   d. It cannot be determined.

GEOMETRY AND ALGEBRA

4. The length of a rectangle is twice its width. If the perimeter of the rectangle is 30 units, what is the width of the rectangle?
   a. 30
   b. 20
   c. 15
   d. 5

5. A circular opening has a diameter of $8\frac{1}{2}$ inches. What is the radius in inches of a circular disk that will exactly fit into the opening?
   a. 17
   b. 8.5
   c. 8
   d. 4.25

6. The radius of a hoop is 10". If you roll the hoop along a straight path through 6 complete revolutions, approximately how far will it roll, in inches? (Use a value of 3.14 for π.)
   a. 31.4
   b. 62.8
   c. 188.4
   d. 376.8

▶ Algebra

Algebra questions do not appear on every test. However, when they do, they typically cover the material you learned in pre-algebra or in the first few months of your high school algebra course. Popular topics for algebra questions include:

- solving equations
- positive and negative numbers
- algebraic expressions

What Is Algebra?

Algebra is a way to express and solve problems using numbers and symbols. These symbols, called **unknowns** or **variables**, are letters of the alphabet that are used to represent numbers.

For example, say you are asked to find out what number, when added to 3, gives you a total of 5. Using algebra, you could express the problem as $x + 3 = 5$. The variable x represents the number you are trying to find.

Here's another example, but this one uses only variables. To find the distance traveled, multiply the rate of travel (speed) by the amount of time traveled: $d = r \times t$. The variable d stands for *distance*, r stands for *rate*, and t stands for *time*.

In algebra, the variables may take on different values. In other words, they *vary*, and that's why they're called *variables*.

GEOMETRY AND ALGEBRA

Operations

Algebra uses the same operations as arithmetic: addition, subtraction, multiplication, and division. In arithmetic, we might say 3 + 4 = 7, while in algebra, we would talk about two numbers whose values we don't know that add up to 7, or $x + y = 7$. Here's how each operation translates to algebra:

ALGEBRAIC OPERATIONS	
The sum of two numbers	$x + y$
The difference of two numbers	$x - y$
The product of two numbers	$x \times y$ or $x \cdot y$ or xy
The quotient of two numbers	$\frac{x}{y}$

Equations

An equation is a mathematical sentence stating that two quantities are equal. For example:

$2x = 10$

$x + 5 = 8$

The idea is to find a replacement for the unknown that will make the sentence true. That's called *solving* the equation. Thus, in the first example, $x = 5$ because $2 \times 5 = 10$. In the second example, $x = 3$ because $3 + 5 = 8$.

Sometimes you can solve an equation by inspection, as with the above examples. Other equations may be more complicated and require a step-by-step solution:

$$\frac{n+2}{4} + 1 = 3$$

The general approach is to consider an equation like a balance scale, with both sides equally balanced. Essentially, whatever you do to one side, you must also do to the other side to maintain the balance. Thus, if you were to add 2 to the left side, you would also have to add 2 to the right side.

Let's apply this *balance* concept to our complicated equation above. Remembering that we want to solve it for n, we must somehow rearrange it so the n is isolated on one side of the equation. Its value will then be on the other side. Looking at the equation, you can see that n has been increased by 2 and then divided by 4 and ultimately added to 1. Therefore, we will undo these operations to isolate n.

Begin by subtracting 1 from both sides of the equation:

$$\frac{n+2}{4} + 1 = 3$$
$$-1 \quad -1$$
$$\frac{n+2}{4} = 2$$

Next, multiply both sides by 4:

$$4 \times \frac{n+2}{4} = 2 \times 4$$
$$n + 2 = 8$$

Finally, subtract 2 from both sides:

$$-2 \quad -2$$

This isolates n and solves the equation:

$$n = 6$$

GEOMETRY AND ALGEBRA

Notice that each operation in the original equation was undone by using the inverse operation. That is, addition was undone by subtraction, and division was undone by multiplication. In general, each operation can be undone by its **inverse**:

ALGEBRAIC INVERSES	
OPERATION	**INVERSE**
Addition	Subtraction
Subtraction	Addition
Multiplication	Division
Division	Multiplication

After you solve an equation, check your work by plugging the answer back into the original equation to make sure it balances. Observe what happens when we plug 6 in for *n*:

$$\frac{6+2}{4} + 1 = 3$$
$$\frac{8}{4} + 1 = 3$$
$$2 + 1 = 3$$
$$3 = 3$$

Solve each equation for *x*:

7. $x + 5 = 12$

8. $3x + 6 = 18$

9. $\frac{1}{4}x = 7$

Positive and Negative Numbers

Positive and negative numbers, also known as **signed** numbers, are best shown as points along the number line:

Numbers to the left of 0 are **negative** and those to the right are **positive**. Zero is neither negative nor positive. If a number is written without a sign, it is assumed to be **positive**. Notice that when you are on the negative side of the number line, numbers with bigger values are actually smaller. For example, −5 is *less than* −2. You come into contact with negative numbers more often than you might think; for example, very cold temperatures are recorded as negative numbers.

GEOMETRY AND ALGEBRA

As you move to the right along the number line, the numbers get larger. Mathematically, to indicate that one number, say 4, is *greater than* another number, say –2, the *greater than* sign (>) is used:

$$4 > -2$$

On the other hand, to say that –2 is *less than* 4, we use the *less than* sign, (<):

$$-2 < 4$$

Arithmetic with Positive and Negative Numbers

The table below illustrates the rules for doing arithmetic with signed numbers. Notice that when a negative number follows an operation (as it does in the second example below), it is enclosed in parentheses to avoid confusion.

RULE	EXAMPLE
ADDITION	
If both numbers have the same sign, just add them. The answer has the same sign as the numbers being added. If both numbers have different signs, subtract the smaller number from the larger. The answer has the same sign as the larger number. If both numbers are the same but have opposite signs, the sum is zero.	3 + 5 = 8 –3 + (–5) = –8 –3 + 5 = 2 3 + (–5) = –2 3 + (–3) = 0
SUBTRACTION	
Change the sign of the number to be subtracted and then add as above.	3 – 5 = 3 + (–5) = –2 –3 – 5 = –3 + (–5) = –8 –3 – (–5) = –3 + 5 = 2
MULTIPLICATION	
Multiply the numbers together. If both numbers have the same sign, the answer is positive; otherwise, it is negative.	3 × 5 = 15 –3 × (–5) = 15 –3 × 5 = –15 3 × (–5) = –15
If one number is zero, the answer is zero.	3 × 0 = 0
DIVISION	
Divide the numbers. If both numbers have the same sign, the answer is positive; otherwise, it is negative.	15 ÷ 3 = 5 –15 ÷ (–3) = 5 15 ÷ (–3) = –5 –15 ÷ 3 = –5
If the top number is zero, the answer is zero.	0 ÷ 3 = 0

GEOMETRY AND ALGEBRA

When more than one arithmetic operation appears, you must know the correct sequence in which to perform the operations. For example, do you know what to do first to calculate $2 + 3 \times 4$? You are right if you said, multiply first. The correct answer is 14. If you add first, you will get the wrong answer of 20. The correct sequence of operations is:

1. parentheses
2. exponents
3. multiplication
4. division
5. addition
6. subtraction

If you remember this saying, you will know the order of operations: **P**lease **E**xcuse **M**y **D**ear **A**unt **S**ally.

Even when signed numbers appear in an equation, the step-by-step solution works exactly as it does for positive numbers. You just have to remember the arithmetic rules for negative numbers. For example, let's solve $14x + 2 = 5$.

1. Subtract 2 from both sides:
$$-14x + 2 = -5$$
$$ -2 -2$$
$$-14x = -7$$

2. Divide both sides by -14: $\quad -14x \div -14 = -7 \div -14$
$$x = \tfrac{1}{2}$$

Now try these problems with signed numbers. Solve for x.

10. $1 - 3 \times (-4) = x$

11. $-3x + 6 = -18$

12. $\frac{x}{-4} + 3 = -7$

Algebraic Expressions

An algebraic expression is a group of numbers, unknowns, and arithmetic operations, like: $3x - 2y$. This one may be translated as, "3 times some number minus 2 times another number." To *evaluate* an algebraic expression, replace each variable with its value. For example, if $x = 5$ and $y = 4$, we would evaluate $3x - 2y$ as follows:

$$3(5) - 2(4) = 15 - 8 = 7$$

GEOMETRY AND ALGEBRA

Evaluate these expressions.

13. $4a + 3b$; $a = 2$ and $b = -1$

14. $3mn - 4m + 2n$; $m = 3$ and $n = -3$

15. $-2x - \frac{1}{2}y + 4z$; $x = 5$, $y = -4$, and $z = 6$

16. The volume of a cylinder is given by the formula $V = \pi r^2 h$, where r is the radius of the base and h is the height of the cylinder. What is the volume of a cylinder with a base radius of 3 and height of 4? (Leave π in your answer.)

17. If $x = 3$, what is the value of $3x - x$?

▶ Answers

Geometry
1. b.
2. c.
3. c.
4. d.
5. d.
6. d.

Algebra
7. 7
8. 4
9. 28
10. 13
11. 8
12. 40
13. 5
14. −45
15. 16
16. 36π
17. 6

LESSON

▶ Word Problems

A word problem tells a story. It may present a situation with numbers and/or unknown information (also called a **variable**). Your job is to translate that word problem into a math problem to solve. Many of the math problems on the ASVAB are word problems. A word problem can include any kind of math, including simple arithmetic, fractions, decimals, percentages—even algebra and geometry. This chapter will give you some helpful hints to use when you try to solve word problems.

▶ Steps to Solving Word Problems

Some simple word problems can be solved by common sense. Most word problems, however, require several steps. Here are some steps to help you solve word problems:

1. **Read a word problem in chunks, rather than straight through.** As you read each chunk, stop to think about what it means. To represent that chunk, take notes, draw a diagram, draw a picture, or write an equation. You may even want to underline important information in each chunk. Repeat this process with

each chunk. Reading a word problem in sections makes the problem easier to understand. Also, you probably won't have to read it again to answer it.

2. **Make a plan of attack.** Figure out what information you already have. Then think about how you're going to use it to solve the problem.
3. **Reread the question** to make sure you've answered the right question after you get your answer. This will help you avoid the careless mistake of answering the wrong question.
4. **Check your work after you get an answer.** In a multiple-choice test, don't assume your answer is correct just because it matches one of the answers given. The most common mistakes are often included in the answer choices. You should always check your work if you have time. Here are a few suggestions:

- Ask yourself if the answer is reasonable: Does it make sense?
- Plug your answer back into the problem: Does it hold together?
- Work the problem a second time, using a different method if you can.
- If a question stumps you, try working the problem backward.

▶ Translating Word Problems

The hardest part of any word problem is translating the story into math. When you read a problem, sometimes you can translate it word for word from English statements into mathematical statements. For many problems, you will write out an equation. An equation is a number sentence that shows two parts that are equal: $45 + 12 = 57$ is a number sentence *and* an equation.

An equation may involve an unknown amount. The unknown is a way of saying that you don't know that part of the equation. Sometimes this unknown amount is represented by a letter. For example, suppose you went shopping and bought a sweater for $45. You also bought a pair of gloves, but you can't remember how much they cost. You do remember that you spent $57 in all. The amount of the gloves is the unknown. You use the letter x to represent the price of the gloves. The equation looks like this: $45 + x = 57$. When you solve the problem, you learn that $x = 12$. The gloves cost $12.

Often, key words in the problem hint at the mathematical operation to be performed and how to translate that story into math. Think of the key word as a word to look for in a word problem that will signal to you what operation to use to set up the equation and solve the problem. Following are some translation tips:

WORD PROBLEMS

EQUALS Key words: *is, are, has*

ENGLISH	MATH
Judi **has** 5 books.	$J = 5$
Bob **is** 18 years old.	$B = 18$
There **are** 7 hats.	$H = 7$

ADDITION Key words: *sum; more, greater, or older than; total; altogether*

ENGLISH	MATH
The **sum** of two numbers is 10.	$X + Y = 10$
Karen has $5 **more** than Sam.	$K = 5 + S$
Judi is 2 years **older** than Tony.	$J = 2 + T$
The **total** of three numbers is 25.	$A + B + C = 25$
The base is 3" **greater than** the height.	$B = 3 + H$
How much do Joan and Tom have **altogether**?	$J + T = ?$

SUBTRACTION Key words: *difference, less or younger than, remain, left over*

ENGLISH	MATH
Jay is 2 years **younger** than Brett.	$J = B - 2$
After Carol ate 3 apples, R apples **remained**.	$R = A - 3$
The **difference** between two numbers is 17.	$X + Y = 17$
Mike has 5 **less** cats than twice the number Jan has.	$M = 2J - 5$

MULTIPLICATION Key words: *of, product, times*

ENGLISH	MATH
Half **of** the boys	$\frac{1}{2} \times B$
The **product** of two numbers is 12.	$A \times B = 12$
20% **of** Matthew's baseball caps	$.20 \times M$

DIVISION Key word: *per*

ENGLISH	MATH
22 miles **per** gallon	22 miles/gallon
15 drops **per** teaspoon	15 drops/teaspoon

Distance Formula: distance = rate × time
Key words are movement words like: *plane, train, boat, car, walk, run, climb, swim,* and also *how far, how long*

ENGLISH	MATH
How far did the plane travel in 4 hours if it averaged 300 miles per hour?	$D = 300 \times 4$ $D = 1{,}200$ miles
Ben **walked** 20 miles in 4 hours. What was his average **speed**?	$20 = r \times 4$ 5 miles per hour $= r$

WORD PROBLEMS

Solving Word Problems Using the Translation Table

Now let's try to solve the following problem using our translation rules.

Example

Carla is reading a novel that has a total of 336 pages. On Friday, she read 35 pages. On Saturday, she read twice the number of pages she read on Friday. How many more pages does she have left to read?

   a. 105
   b. 231
   c. 266
   d. 301

Here's how we marked up the question. Notice how we underlined key phrases and we used letters to represent words: *t* for total, *F* instead of Friday, and *S* instead of Saturday.

Carla is reading a novel that has a <u>total of 336</u> pages. On Friday, she read <u>35 pages</u>. On Saturday, she read <u>twice</u> the number of pages she read on Friday. <u>How many more pages</u> does she have <u>left</u> to read?

$t = 336$
$F = 35$
$S = 2 \times 35$
$? = \text{left}$

The words *more* and *left* hint at both addition and subtraction. The word *twice* (meaning *two times more*) hints at multiplication.

What we know:

- Carla read 35 pages one day.
- Carla read 2 times 35 pages the next day.
- The book has a total of 336 pages.

The question itself: How many more pages does she have left to read?

Plan of attack:

- Find the number of pages she has already read.
- Find out how many pages are left.

Solution

You know how many pages Carla read on Friday: 35. If you want to find out how many pages she read on Saturday, you will use multiplication: $2 \times 35 = 70$. Next, you will use addition to find out how many pages she has already read: $35 + 70 = 105$. But the question asks, "How many pages does she have left to read?" The word *left* indicates that you will use subtraction: $366 - 105 = 231$. So to answer this question, you must take three steps.

You must use three operations: addition, subtraction, and multiplication.

Step 1: $2 \times 35 = 70$
Step 2: $35 + 70 = 105$
Step 3: $366 - 105 = 231$
Answer: Carla has 231 pages left to read.

Check Your Work

Check your work by plugging your answer back into the original problem. See if the whole thing makes sense:

Carla is reading a novel that has a total of 336 pages. On Friday, she read 35 pages. On Saturday, she read 70 pages. She has 231 pages left to read.

Carla has already read 105 pages (25 + 70). If she reads 231 more (105 + 231 = 336), she will have read all 336 pages.

WORD PROBLEMS

Practice Word Problems

Practice using the translation table to help you solve problems that require you to work with basic arithmetic. Answers are at the end of the chapter.

1. Joan went shopping with $100 and returned home with only $18.42. How much money did she spend?
   a. $81.58
   b. $72.68
   c. $72.58
   d. $71.68

2. Mark invited ten friends to a party. Each friend brought three guests. How many people came to the party, excluding Mark?
   a. 3
   b. 10
   c. 30
   d. 40

3. The office secretary can type 80 words per minute on his word processor. How many minutes will it take him to type a report containing 760 words?
   a. 8
   b. 8.5
   c. 9
   d. 9.5

4. Mr. Wallace is writing a budget request to upgrade his personal computer system. He wants to purchase 4 mb of RAM, which will cost $100, two new software programs at $350 each, a tape backup system for $249, and an additional tape for $25. What is the total amount Mr. Wallace should write on his budget request?
   a. $724
   b. $974
   c. $1,049
   d. $1,074

Fractions

5. The length of a table plus $\frac{1}{5}$ of its length is 36 inches. How long is the table, in inches?
   a. 30
   b. 40
   c. 42
   d. 45

6. An outside wall is $5\frac{7}{8}$ inches thick. The wall consists of $\frac{1}{2}$ inch of drywall and $3\frac{3}{4}$ inches of insulation, and $\frac{5}{8}$ inch of wall sheathing. The remaining thickness is siding. How thick is the siding?
   a. $\frac{1}{8}$ inch
   b. $\frac{1}{4}$ inch
   c. $\frac{1}{2}$ inch
   d. 1 inch

WORD PROBLEMS

7. A certain test is scored by adding 1 point for each correct answer and subtracting $\frac{1}{4}$ of a point for each incorrect answer. If Jan answered 31 questions correctly and 9 questions incorrectly, what was her score?
  a. $28\frac{3}{4}$
  b. $28\frac{1}{4}$
  c. 26
  d. $22\frac{1}{4}$

8. Bart took a taxi $\frac{1}{4}$ of the distance to Mandy's house. He took a bus for $\frac{1}{3}$ of the distance to her house. Finally, he walked the remaining 5 miles to her house. How many miles did Bart travel in all?
  a. 9
  b. 10
  c. $11\frac{3}{4}$
  d. 12

9. Ursula can walk $3\frac{1}{2}$ miles per hour. If she walks for $2\frac{1}{4}$ hours, how far will she walk, in miles?
  a. $5\frac{3}{4}$
  b. $6\frac{1}{4}$
  c. $7\frac{7}{8}$
  d. 18

Decimals

10. At a certain discount store, if you purchase five pairs of socks, you get one pair of socks free. If one pair of socks costs $1.25, and Jeff left the store with 18 pairs of socks, how much did he spend?
  a. $18.75
  b. 20.00
  c. $21.25
  d. $22.50

11. Roland has a stack of small boxes, all the same size. If the stack measures 55.5 centimeters high and each box is 9.25 centimeters high, how many boxes does he have?
  a. 5
  b. 6
  c. 7
  d. 8

12. Selma bought four items at the grocery store that cost $1.98, $2.65, $4.29, and $6.78. She gave the clerk a $20 bill. How much change did she receive?
  a. $3.30
  b. $4.30
  c. $4.40
  d. $15.70

13. At a price of $.82 per pound, which of the following comes closest to the cost of a turkey weighing $9\frac{1}{4}$ pounds?
  a. $6.80
  b. $7.00
  c. $7.60
  d. $8.20

Percents

14. If the price of a bottle of maple syrup is reduced from $4 to $3, by what percent is the price reduced?
 a. $\frac{1}{4}$%
 b. $\frac{1}{3}$%
 c. 1%
 d. 25%

15. A credit card company charges $12\frac{1}{4}$% interest on the unpaid balance. If Mona has an unpaid balance of $220, how much interest will she be charged for one month?
 a. $2.75
 b. $14.4
 c. $24.00
 d. $26.95

16. Fifteen percent of the 3,820 employees at TechnoCorps were hired this year. How many of TechnoCorps employees were NOT hired this year?
 a. 573
 b. 1,910
 c. 3,247
 d. 3,805

17. Gilbert won 12 out of the 19 tennis matches he played in. What percent of his matches did he lose, rounded to the nearest percent?
 a. 37%
 b. 39%
 c. 59%
 d. 63%

▶ Answers

1. a.
2. d.
3. d.
4. d.
5. a.
6. d.
7. a.
8. d.
9. c.
10. a.
11. b.
12. b.
13. c.
14. d.
15. d.
16. c.
17. a.

SECTION 3
Reading Comprehension for the Paragraph Comprehension Subtest

READING IS A vital skill. Understanding written materials is critical for taking the ASVAB—after all, you can't understand the questions if you don't read well—but it is also critical for any military job. Memos, policies, procedures, reports—these are all things you will be expected to understand if you enlist in the armed services. That is why the ASVAB attempts to measure how well applicants understand what they read.

The Paragraph Comprehension subtest of the ASVAB contains multiple-choice questions based on brief passages. These questions test your ability to understand what you read. If you do not consider yourself a strong reader, take plenty of time to review the strategies in the following lessons. You should also complete all the practice exercises, so that you can increase your score on this important subtest.

READING COMPREHENSION FOR THE PARAGRAPH COMPREHENSION SUBTEST

▶ Active Reading

Good readers are active readers. They see reading as an involved process. That's why they understand so much of what they read. To be an active reader you should:

1. **Write when you read.** Writing while you read can really help you absorb information better. Try to:
   - **underline key words and ideas** to help important information stand out so that you can remember it later and summarize it.
   - **circle and look up unfamiliar words and phrases**—you need to know what all the words in a sentence mean in order to completely understand what you are reading.
   - **list any questions and comments you might have.** As you read, you are bound to have questions. You're likely to have reactions to the reading as well. Writing your questions and thoughts makes you think about what you read, and that means you will better understand the material.
2. **Pay close attention when you read.** Take note of the details in sentences and passages to find clues that help you better understand the writer's ideas. Making observations and finding these clues are essential because your observations are what lead you to logical inferences about what you read. Inferences are conclusions based on reason, fact, or evidence. If you misunderstand what you read, it is often because you haven't looked closely enough at the text.

▶ Types of Reading Comprehension Questions

You have probably encountered reading comprehension questions before, where you were given a passage to read and then required to answer relevant multiple-choice questions about it. This kind of question has an advantage for you as a test taker: You don't have to know anything about the topic of the passage because you're being tested only on the information the passage provides.

The disadvantage is that you have to know where and how to find that information quickly in an unfamiliar text. This makes it easy to select one of the wrong answer choices, especially since they're designed to mislead you.

The best way to do well on this passage/question format is to be very familiar with the kinds of questions that are typically asked on the test. Questions most frequently ask you to:

1. identify a specific fact or detail in the passage
2. uncover the main idea of the passage
3. make an inference based on the passage
4. define a vocabulary word from the passage

The following list of important words will greatly help you to answer reading comprehension questions. These words will allow you to become a better, more active reader.

READING COMPREHENSION FOR THE PARAGRAPH COMPREHENSION SUBTEST

▶ Reading Comprehension Glossary

Argument	a discussion aimed at proving something to be true; a claim supported by reasons or evidence
Basic Information	core facts or data, essential knowledge or ideas
Cause	a person or thing that makes something happen or creates an effect
Chronology	the order in which things happen
Compare	to examine in order to find similarities between two or more items
Conclusion	belief or opinion based on reasoning
Connotation	the suggested or implied meaning of a word; its emotional impact
Context	the words and ideas surrounding a word that help give it its meaning
Contrast	to show the differences between two or more items
Effect	a change created by an action or cause
Emotional	drawn from the emotions; based on strong mental feelings
Fact	something known for certain to be true
Formality	the quality of being proper, ceremonious
General	broad, wide, nonspecific; applying to most or all
Imply	to hint or suggest without stating directly
Indifferent	uncaring, showing no interest
Logical	according to reason; based on evidence or good common sense
Main Idea	the thought that holds a passage together
Narrator	the person who tells the story
Objective	unaffected by the thoughts, feelings, and experiences of the writer
Observant	paying careful attention
Observation	something seen or noticed
Opinion	something believed to be true, but that cannot be proven to be true
Point of View	the person or position through which you see things
Rank	position or value in relation to others in a group
Reason	a motive or grounds for something; good sense or judgment

READING COMPREHENSION FOR THE PARAGRAPH COMPREHENSION SUBTEST

Sentence Structure	the size and parts of a sentence
Specific	particular, exact
Style	the way of doing something, such as writing or speaking; the manner in which something is done
Subject	whom or what the passage is about
Subjective	based on the thoughts, feelings, and experiences of the writer
Tone	the mood or attitude conveyed by words or speech
Topic Sentence	the sentence that states the main idea
Transitions	words and phrases that link ideas and how the ideas relate to each other

LESSON

Reading Comprehension Basics

This lesson will help you learn how to become an active reader. You will master a few basic skills to build a strong reading foundation. By the end of this lesson (and with a little practice), you should be able to:

1. uncover the basic facts in a passage
2. find the main idea of a passage
3. decipher what words mean without a dictionary
4. recognize the difference between fact and opinion

▶ Grasping the Basic Information

The first thing you need to do when you read anything is to grasp the basic information. This includes the who, what, when, where, how, and why. What does the passage tell you? What happens? To whom? When? Where? How? Why?

READING COMPREHENSION BASICS

The questions you ask yourself will change from reading to reading, but the idea is always the same: You need to find the basic information. Being observant while you read will help you find this information.

The following is a short paragraph that could be from a local newspaper article. Read it carefully and actively. As you read, look for the basic facts and think about the who, what, when, where, why, and how.

> Yesterday the house of Mr. and Mrs. Jason White was robbed. The thieves entered the house at 13 Elm Avenue around noon. Mr. White and his wife, Alison, were not home. The house had an expensive security system linked to the local police station, but no alarms went off at the precinct. The robbery wasn't discovered until Mrs. White came home at 3:45 P.M. Police say that the thieves disconnected the security system. The thieves stole all of the Whites's furniture, jewelry, office equipment, and artwork. Mrs. White is an art appraiser. She values the stolen property at $1.6 million.

Reading actively should help you find the basic information in this passage. Here are some questions you could ask to find the facts:

1. What happened? _____
2. When did it happen? _____
3. Where did it happen? _____
4. How did it happen? _____
5. Who discovered the theft? _____
6. When was the theft discovered? _____
7. What was stolen? _____
8. How much is the stolen property worth? _____

Here's how this passage might look after an active reading. The basic facts have been underlined. There are notes in the margins. There is also a definition for the word appraise.

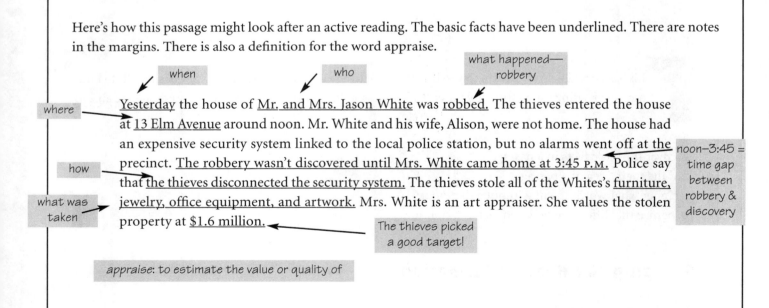

94

READING COMPREHENSION BASICS

Here are the answers to the questions:

1. What happened? *The White's house was robbed.*
2. When did it happen? *Yesterday*
3. Where did it happen? *13 Elm Avenue*
4. How did it happen? *The thieves disconnected the security system.*
5. Who discovered the theft? *Mrs. White*
6. When was the theft discovered? *At 3:45 in the afternoon*
7. What was stolen? *Their furniture, jewelry, office equipment, and artwork*
8. How much is the stolen property worth? *$1.6 million*

This is the basic information in the paragraph. You could ask more questions and there is no rule to tell you how many questions you should ask yourself. What you need to know depends on what kind of text you're reading. Are you reading a magazine article for pleasure about an athlete? Then just a handful of questions should do. But, if it's a chapter in a history book, or a passage on the ASVAB, it has important information that you will need to understand and remember. So in this case, ask yourself more questions.

▶ Practice 1

In the following practice exercise, read the passage below carefully and actively. Then answer the questions that follow. Asnwers are found on page 101.

Remember to be an active reader. Circle and look up unfamiliar words, underline key words and ideas, and write questions and comments in the margins. Ask yourself questions as you read. When you are done, you can check your answers at the end of the lesson.

The U.S. Postal Service is more efficient than ever. Mail used to take months to arrive. It was delivered by horse or by foot. Now trucks, trains, and planes transport it around the country in days or hours. First-class mail arrives in three days or less. Urgent mail can move even faster. Priority Mail is guaranteed to go anywhere in the United States in three days or less. Express Mail will get your package there overnight.

Questions

1. What word is used to describe the current U.S. Postal Service? _____

2. How long did it take mail to arrive in the past? _____

3. Other than trucks and planes, how else is mail moved today? _____

4. Can urgent mail be sent in less than three days? _____

5. How long does Priority Mail take? _____

6. How long does Express Mail take? _____

▶ Finding the Main Idea

The **main idea** is the thought that holds the passage together. The *why* of the passage. A good reader asks himself, "Why did the author write this? What idea does he or she want me to understand?" Asking yourself these questions will help lead you to the main idea of a passage.

The Difference between Subject and Main Idea

People often confuse the **subject** with the main idea, but there is an important difference. To see the difference, take another look at the passage about the postal system.

> The U.S. Postal Service is more efficient than ever. Mail used to take months to arrive. It was delivered by horse or by foot. Now trucks, trains, and planes transport it around the country in days or hours. First-class mail arrives in three days or less. Urgent mail can move even faster. Priority Mail is guaranteed to go anywhere in the United States in three days or less. Express Mail will get your package there overnight.

Reading tests often ask, "What is the main idea of this passage?" For the passage above, you might answer, "the post office." But you would be making a common mistake. The passage is *about* the post office, but the post office is not the main idea. Instead, the post office is the subject of the passage. The subject is who or what the passage is about. The main idea, on the other hand, says something about the subject.

Look back at the paragraph about the postal service, once again. The subject is the post office. Read the passage carefully and look for the idea that makes a claim about the subject. Remember, the idea should be general and it should hold together the whole paragraph. Now answer the following question:

> Which sentence best summarizes the main idea of the passage?
> **a.** Express Mail is a good way to send urgent mail.
> **b.** Mail service today is very effective.
> **c.** First-class mail usually takes three days or less.
> **d.** Mail used to take months to arrive.

All four options make a claim about mail services, but **a, c,** and **d** are too specific to be the main idea. None of these answers covers all of the ideas in the paragraph.

Only choice **b** is general enough to cover the whole paragraph. All of the other sentences support the idea that mail service is very effective. Each sentence offers proof for that idea. The writer's motive is to show that the post office is better than ever. That main idea is stated in the first sentence, and the rest of the sentences support that idea.

The main idea of a passage, then, makes a claim about its subject. But the main idea does more than that. It also holds the whole passage together. All of the other sentences in the passage must support that idea. They usually give specific examples or explanations. In a way, the main idea is like a net over the passage. It is the general idea that covers all of the specific ideas in the paragraph.

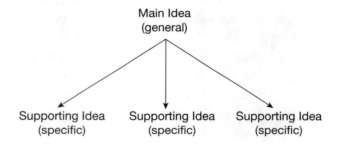

The main idea is both a claim about the subject and the general idea that binds all of the ideas in the passage.

▶ Topic Sentences

The **topic sentence** is a claim about the subject. It is usually a claim that needs support or proof. A topic sentence clearly states the main idea, and it must be general enough to cover all of the ideas in the passage.

READING COMPREHENSION BASICS

▶ Practice 2

Look at the following paragraph. Read it carefully and then underline the sentence that best states the topic sentence. You can check your answer at the end of the lesson.

Erik always played cops and robbers when he was a boy. Now he's a police officer. Lauren always pretended to be a doctor as a little girl. Today she's a pediatrician. Kara always played store. Now she owns her own clothing store. Some lucky people have always known what they want to do with their lives.

▶ Introducing Specific Examples

Readers need to see that the claim made in the topic sentence is true. That's what the other supporting sentences in the postal service paragraph do. They show readers that the postal service is more efficient than ever.

Supporting sentences often begin with signal words that tell you they are about to introduce specific examples. Sentences that begin with these words and phrases are usually not topic sentences but rather supporting sentences, introducing specific examples. Here are some words and phrases that often introduce specific examples.

for example	furthermore	in addition
in particular	some	others
for instance		

Sometimes you might have trouble finding the main idea. You can try crossing out sentences that begin with these words. Then you will have fewer sentences to choose from, and the topic sentences should be easier to find.

▶ Defining Words in Context

As you read, you will often see unfamiliar words, or words you cannot define. You might have a dictionary, then you can look up those words. But what if you don't have a dictionary? How can you understand what you're reading if you don't know what the words mean?

You can often figure out what a word means if you look at its **context**—the words and ideas surrounding a word that help supply its meaning. Reading comprehension tests, like the one on the ASVAB, often test your ability to find the meaning of words based on the context of the passage.

Finding Meaning in Context

Sometimes you can't understand an entire sentence, or group of sentences, if you don't understand one key word. For example, look at the following sentence.

The new policy will *substantially* cut employee benefits.

Can you fully understand the sentence without knowing what *substantially* means? As an employee, you will want to know what *substantially* means. How much will your benefits be cut? This is an important question. Is *substantially* a little or a lot? There are not enough clues in this sentence; to figure out what the word means, you need more context.

Here's the same sentence in a paragraph.

The new policy will substantially cut employee benefits. Employees will lose their dental coverage. Regular doctor check-ups will no longer be covered. In addition, psychiatric coverage will be cut from six visits to two.

You should be able to figure out what *substantially* means now.

Substantially means
a. just barely.
b. a little, but not too much.
c. small.
d. a lot.

The answer is choice **d**, *a lot*. The paragraph describes a big cut in coverage. Both dental care and regular check-ups will no longer be covered and psychiatric care will be cut by two-thirds. These are serious cutbacks. You may have also noticed that *substantially* is similar to the word *substance*. Something that has substance is weighty or solid. It is not light. Your knowledge of related words can also help you define words in context.

▶ Practice 3

Read the following sentences carefully. Use context to determine what the italicized words mean. Then circle the correct meanings. Check your answers at the end of the lesson.

1. I accidentally told Nell about her surprise party. What a stupid *blunder*!
   A *blunder* is
   a. a jerk.
   b. an idea.
   c. a mistake.
   d. a get-together.

2. Our successful salespeople share one personality *trait*: honesty.
   A *trait* is
   a. an aspect.
   b. a disorder.
   c. a difference.
   d. a similarity.

3. Please return the pink copy. *Retain* the yellow copy for your records.
   To *retain* means
   a. to copy.
   b. to throw away.
   c. to read.
   d. to keep.

▶ Practice 4

Provide context for the words below. Write a sentence or two for each word. The sentences should show the reader what the words mean. Check your answers at the end of the lesson.

Example:

<u>word</u>: glimpse
<u>meaning</u>: to catch a quick view of
<u>context</u>: I'm not sure what he looked like. I only glimpsed the man's face before he disappeared around the corner.

1. <u>word</u>: mundane
   <u>meaning</u>: dull, boring, routine
   <u>context</u>:

2. <u>word</u>: teem
   <u>meaning</u>: to be full of, to be present in large numbers
   <u>context</u>:

▶ The Difference between Fact and Opinion

Sometimes people tell you what they *know* is true—they are telling you facts. Other times they tell you what they *think* is true—they are telling you opinions.

READING COMPREHENSION BASICS

A **fact** is:

- something *known* for certain to have happened
- something *known* for certain to be true
- something *known* for certain to exist

An **opinion**, on the other hand, is:

- something *believed* to have happened
- something *believed* to be true
- something *believed* to exist

The key difference between fact and opinion is the difference between *knowing* and *believing*. Opinions are often based on facts, but opinions are still what people think or feel. They are not what people know. You can argue about an opinion, but you can't argue about a fact. In other words, opinions are debatable while facts are not.

Using Facts to Support Opinions

People can have opinions about almost anything. What's important is that they support their opinions. An opinion supported by facts is a reasonable opinion. In fact, that's mostly what you read about. Writers make a claim about their subject, and that claim is often an opinion. Then they offer facts to support their opinion.

Think about your own opinions. You could write a topic sentence about your friend Margarita:

Margarita is a good friend.

This is a good topic sentence. It makes a claim about its subject, Margarita, and it's also an opinion. It is something you could argue about. After all, someone could make an opposite claim:

Margarita is a bad friend.

This is another good topic sentence. It's also another opinion. A good writer will now show readers that this is a reasonable opinion. How? By offering supporting facts.

Margarita is a good friend. She always asks me how I am. If I have a problem, she is always willing to listen to me talk about it. For my last birthday, she organized a surprise party for me and invited all my friends. She even baked me a birthday cake.

The topic sentence states an opinion and the rest of the sentences support that opinion. They offer facts about Margarita. This makes it an effective paragraph. Now, here is a writer who doesn't support his opinion well.

Margarita is a bad friend. I don't think that her jokes are funny, and she doesn't seem to care about me at all. And, she has stupid ideas about politics.

The first paragraph about Margarita is much better because it's not just an opinion. It's an opinion supported by facts. The second paragraph is all opinion. Every sentence is arguable, and the sentences show what the author *thinks* is true, not what is *known* to be true. The second paragraph doesn't include specific facts to show why Margarita is a bad friend, it includes only what the author *thinks* about Margarita.

▶ Practice 5

Read the following claims carefully. Are they fact or opinion? Write an F in the blank if the claim is a fact and an O in the blank if the claim is an opinion. When you are done, you can check your answers at the end of the lesson.

_____ **1.** The summer Olympics are held every two years.

_____ **2.** The Olympics are fun to watch.

_____ **3.** The Olympics should be held every year.

_____ **4.** The 1996 Summer Olympics were held in Atlanta, Georgia.

_____ **5.** The long jump is the most exciting Olympic event.

▶ Review

So far you know how to get the basic information from a passage. You know that asking *who, what, when, where, why,* and *how* will help you gather important information from what you are reading. You can also tell the difference between the subject, who or what the passage is about, and the main idea of a passage. You know that the main idea makes a claim about the subject and is general enough to hold the passage together. The other sentences in the passage all support the main idea, which is often expressed in a topic sentence. In addition, you know how to decipher what words mean from the context. You also know how to look for clues in the words and sentences around unfamiliar words. Finally, you learned that a fact is something *known* to be true. While an opinion is something *believed* to be true. Many main ideas are opinions. Good writers use facts to support their opinions.

▶ Review Practice

Now you can put all the skills you just learned together by reading the following longer passage. Read the following passage and answer the questions. Check your answers at the end of the lesson.

Bicycles

Today, bicycles are so common that it's hard to believe they haven't always been around. But two hundred years ago, bicycles didn't exist, and the first bicycle, invented in Germany in 1818, was nothing like our bicycles today. It was made of wood and did not even have pedals. Since then, however, numerous innovations and improvements in design have made the bicycle one of the most popular means of recreation and transportation around the world.

In 1839, Kirkpatrick Macmillan, a Scottish blacksmith, dramatically improved upon the original bicycle design. Macmillan's machine had tires with iron rims to keep them from getting worn down. He also used foot-operated cranks similar to pedals so his bicycle could be ridden at a quick pace. It didn't look much like a modern bicycle, though, because its back wheel was substantially larger than its front wheel. In 1861, the French Michaux brothers took the evolution of the bicycle a step further by inventing an improved crank mechanism.

Ten years later, James Starley, an English inventor, revolutionized bicycle design. He made the front wheel many times larger than the back wheel, put a gear on the pedals to make the bicycle more efficient, and lightened the wheels by using wire spokes. Although this bicycle was much lighter and less tiring to ride, it was still clumsy, extremely top-heavy, and ridden mostly for entertainment.

It wasn't until 1874 that the first truly modern bicycle appeared on the scene. Invented by another Englishman, H.J. Lawson, the "safety bicycle" would look familiar to today's cyclists. This bicycle had equal-sized wheels, which made it less prone to toppling over. Lawson also attached a chain to the pedals to drive the rear wheel. With these improvements, the bicycle became extremely popular and useful for transportation. Today they are built, used, and enjoyed all over the world.

READING COMPREHENSION BASICS

1. The main idea of this passage is best expressed in which sentence?
   a. Today, bicycles are so common that it's hard to believe they haven't always been around.
   b. It wasn't until 1874 that the first truly modern bicycle appeared on the scene.
   c. Since then, however, numerous innovations and improvements in design have made the bicycle one of the most popular means of recreation and transportation around the world.
   d. Today they are built, used, and enjoyed all over the world.

2. Which of the following would be the best title for this passage?
   a. Bicycles Are Better
   b. A Ride through the History of Bicycles
   c. Cycle Your Way to Fitness
   d. The Popularity of Bicycles

3. Which sentence best expresses the main idea of the second paragraph?
   a. Macmillan was a great inventor.
   b. Macmillan's bike didn't look much like our modern bikes.
   c. Macmillan's bike could be ridden quickly.
   d. Macmillan made important changes in bicycle design.

4. An *innovation* is
   a. a new way of doing something.
   b. a design.
   c. a repair.
   d. a clever person.

5. Macmillan added iron rims to the tires of his bicycle to
   a. add weight to the bicycle.
   b. make the tires last longer.
   c. make the ride less bumpy.
   d. make the ride less tiring.

6. The first person to use a gear system on bicycles was
   a. H.J. Lawson.
   b. Kirkpatrick Macmillan.
   c. The Michaux brothers.
   d. James Starley.

▶ Answers

Practice 1
1. efficient
2. months
3. trains
4. yes
5. three days or less
6. overnight

Practice 2
You should have underlined the last sentence: "Some lucky people have always known what they want to do with their lives." This sentence is a good topic sentence. It states the idea that holds the whole passage together. The first six sentences are specific examples of that idea. Thus, they all support the main idea. This time, the topic sentence is at the end of the paragraph.

Practice 3
1. c. The writer wasn't supposed to tell Nell about the surprise birthday party. Thus, a *blunder* is a mistake.
2. a. Honesty isn't a *problem*, so b can't be the answer. The passage says that the salespeople have this *trait* in common, so c can't be correct either. The only word that makes sense in the sentence is a, *aspect*.
3. d. You would want to keep a copy for your records.

Practice 4
Answers will vary. Here are some examples:

1. My job is very mundane. I do the same thing every day.
2. We left the picnic basket open. When we got back, it was teeming with ants.

Practice 5
1. F
2. O. This is clearly something arguable. Many people enjoy watching the Olympics. But there are others who do not think it is fun. This is a matter of opinion.
3. O. Again, this is clearly something arguable.
4. F
5. O. There are many events at the Olympics. People have different opinions about which event they like best.

Review Practice
1. c. This is the only sentence general enough to encompass all of the ideas in the passage. Each paragraph describes the innovations that led to the modern design of the bicycle, and this design has made it popular around the world.
2. b. The essay describes the history of the bicycle, from its invention in 1818 to its modern design.
3. d. Macmillan may have been a great inventor, but this paragraph only describes his innovations in bicycle design. The first sentence in this paragraph expresses this main idea in a clear topic sentence. The rest of the paragraph provides specific examples of the improvements he made in bicycle design.
4. a. An innovation is a new way of doing something. The first clue is in the third sentence, which describes the first bicycle—"it was made of wood and did not even have pedals." Clearly, bicycles have changed dramatically. Other clues can be found in the following paragraphs, which describe the various changes made to bicycle design. Each bicycle designer devised a new way of building a bicycle.
5. b. Since the question is asking for a specific fact about Macmillan's design, you should know to look in the second paragraph. Then you can find the sentence with the key words, iron rims—the second sentence—to find the correct answer.
6. d. If you highlighted the various innovations, then all you have to do is scan the highlighted parts of the passage. If not, paragraph 3 states, "Starley . . . put a gear on the pedals."

LESSON 9 ▶ Structure

Understanding structure—how writers organize their ideas—will help you to comprehend what you read better. Writers must decide how to arrange their sentences and ideas. They decide which ideas go where, and they must choose how to move from one idea to another. Most writers organize their ideas in four patterns that help them effectively express their ideas:

- Time Order
- Order of Importance
- Compare and Contrast
- Cause and Effect

Reading will become easier for you as you learn to recognize these four patterns.

STRUCTURE

▶ Time Order

There are many ways to tell a story. Often, though, stories begin with what happened first. The rest of the story follows the order in which the events occurred. Time order is also called **chronological order**—the order in which things happen.

Time Order and Transitions

Much of what you read is in time order. Newspaper and magazine articles are usually arranged this way—so are meeting minutes and directions. For example, look at the following paragraph. It resembles something you might see in a company newsletter:

> Our employee awards dinner was a success. To begin, President Mike Smith announced the award for Perfect Attendance. Carlos Feliciano and Yelena Grishov were the winners. The second award was for Most Dedicated Employee. Jennifer Steele received this award. Then Mr. Smith made an announcement. He and his wife are expecting their first child. Afterward, Vice President Jane Wu offered a toast. Next Mr. Smith gave the final award for Best New Idea. This award went to Karen Hunt. Finally, Mr. Smith ended the event with another surprise: He announced a 2% raise for all employees.

This paragraph describes what happened from start to finish. The writer used transitions to help you follow the order of events. **Transitions** allow writers to move from one idea to another. They also show readers the relationship between ideas. For example, transitions may show that one event came before another. That's how they work in this passage. Notice the transitions *to begin, second, then, afterward, next,* and *finally* in the paragraph. They keep the events in chronological order. Thus, transitions are important tools to help readers follow ideas in the paragraph.

These transitions signal the chronology in a paragraph:

first	*second*
third, etc.	*next*
now	*then*
when	*soon*
before	*after*
during	*while*
meanwhile	*in the meantime*
immediately	*suddenly*
at last	*eventually*
finally	*later*
before long	*shortly*
as soon as	*after a while*

Transitions are one clue to look for to help you figure out the order of events in a passage. These words also help readers understand the relationship between ideas. Knowing the order of events is often important.

▶ Practice 1

The following is a list of transitions. Choose the ones that best fit into the paragraph. Write them in the blanks of the paragraph. Check your answers at the end of this lesson.

when
as soon as
yesterday
then
a moment later
right away

____ I went to work early to get some extra filing done. ____ I got there, the phone started ringing. ____ my boss walked in. ____ he asked me to type a letter. ____ he asked me to set up a conference call. ____ I looked at my watch, it was already 11:00.

STRUCTURE

▶ Order of Importance

Another way to present ideas is in order of importance. Once you understand this structure you will see which ideas are most important in what you read.

Ideas can be organized by rank. Using this method, the first idea listed isn't the one that happened first, but rather it's the idea that is the most, or least, important. If writers start with the most important idea, then they would continue to the least important idea. Or they could do the reverse and start with the least important idea and build up to the idea that is most important. Writers usually choose their structure according to their purpose. And that structure affects how you understand what you read.

Most Important to Least Important

Sometimes passages begin with the most important idea. This often happens in newspaper articles. Readers want to know the most important facts right away: "Student protesters shut down the campus at UCLA today" or "City officials approved a tax cut." Writers choose this order so that readers will remember what they read first.

Here's a passage organized from the most important to the least important idea. Read it actively.

> There are many ways to make tax time easier. The most important thing you can do is keep good records. Keep all of your pay stubs, receipts, and bank statements in a neat folder. When you're ready to prepare your tax form, all of your paperwork will be in one place. The second thing you can do is start early. Start filling out the forms as soon as they arrive in the mail. If you run into problems, you'll have plenty of time to solve them. Finally, read the directions. This act can keep you from redoing the form because you did it wrong the first time. It can also keep you from making mistakes.

The passage begins with a clear topic sentence. Then it offers three tax-time tips. The writer gives the most important tip first. "The most important thing you can do is keep good records."

What is the second-most important thing you can do to make tax time easier? The writer started with the most important thing, meaning that the ideas are organized from most to least important. Thus, the second most important tip should come right after the first. The second best thing to do is "start early."

Finally, what's the third-most important tip the writer offers? The answer, of course is the last tip. You should "read the directions."

Least Important to Most Important

Some writers organize ideas the opposite way. They don't start with the most important idea. Instead, they end with it. This order offers writers three advantages. First, readers are left with a strong conclusion. Second, this order makes use of what is called the *snowball effect*. Like a snowball rolling down a hill, the writer's ideas build and build. They get more and more important. Each idea builds on the ones that come before it. Third, starting with the least important idea creates suspense. Readers will be waiting to learn that final important idea.

You can often expect to see this structure in an argument. In an argument, the end is usually where the last point has the most impact.

▶ Practice 2

Following is a list of reasons for reading more often. If you were to put these reasons in a paragraph, how would you organize them? First, rank the reasons in order of importance. Then rank them according to how you would present them.

STRUCTURE

Five Reasons to Read More Often:

- You will broaden your vocabulary.
- You will improve your reading comprehension.
- You will increase your reading speed.
- You will develop a better understanding of yourself and others.
- You will learn new information and ideas.

Order of Importance to You

1. _____
2. _____
3. _____
4. _____
5. _____

Order of Presentation

1. _____
2. _____
3. _____
4. _____
5. _____

In which order did you present your ideas? Most important to least important, or least important to most important? Either structure will work well with these ideas. Some writers want to hit their readers with what's most important at the beginning. Then they'll be sure to catch their readers' attention. Or they may want to save their best ideas for last. That way, readers build up to the most important idea.

Now that you've organized the ideas about reading, put them into a paragraph. Add a topic sentence and transitions to the sentences listed.

_____
_____
_____
_____
_____

▶ Compare and Contrast

People spend a lot of time thinking about similarities and differences. When they want to explain similarities, they often compare the items. That will show how things are similar. Likewise, when they want to show how things are different, they contrast them to emphasize the differences between the items.

How Comparing and Contrasting Works

When people **compare** and **contrast**, they show how two things are similar or different. This helps others to judge the things that are being compared. For example, by comparing a cup of coffee to mud, you can give someone an idea how the coffee looks and tastes.

Writers use comparison and contrast for the same reason. When you read, you can see how two or more things measure up side by side. What do they have in common? What sets them apart?

Read the following passage carefully to see how the technique of compare and contrast works.

Being an assistant is a lot like being a parent. A child is dependent upon her parent. Your boss is dependent on you. Children must ask for permission before they go out. Similarly, your boss will come to you for permission, too. You keep track of her schedule. "Can I have a meeting on Tuesday at 3:30?" your boss might ask. You'll also clean up after your boss. Just as a parent tucks toys away at the end of the day, you'll file papers, put things back into drawers, and tidy up the office. A parent protects his or her children from danger. Likewise, you'll find yourself protecting your boss from dangers like angry callers and clients. But there is one big difference. Children grow more independent each year. Your boss will grow more dependent on you as the years pass.

STRUCTURE

Two things are being compared and contrasted here: a parent and an assistant. The writer lists four similarities between parents and assistants:

1. Bosses depend upon assistants like children depend upon their parents.
2. Bosses ask permission from their assistants to do certain things just as children ask permission from their parents.
3. Assistants clean up after their bosses like parents clean up after children.
4. Assistants protect their bosses like parents protect their children.

Then the writer points out one difference between assistants and parents. Children grow less and less dependent upon their parents. Meanwhile, bosses grow more and more dependent upon their assistants.

Remember, writers always have a motive. So when you come across compare and contrast passages, ask yourself why the author is comparing those items. What does the writer want you to get from the comparison? This comparison makes readers see assistants in a new way. That's one of the values of this structure.

Transitions in Comparison and Contrast

Did you notice the transitions in the paragraph about assistants and parents? Some transitions told you that the writer was comparing (showing a similarity). Others told you that the writer was contrasting (showing a difference). Read the passage again. As you read it this time, underline the transitions.

There are several transitions that show comparison and contrast. You should have underlined *like, similarly, also, just as, likewise,* and *but*. Following is a more complete list of transitional words and phrases.

WORDS THAT HELP YOU COMPARE	
similarly	in the same way
likewise	in a like manner
like	just as, just like
also	much as, much like

WORDS THAT HELP YOU CONTRAST	
but	on the contrary
however	on the other hand
yet	nevertheless
conversely	

▶ Practice 3

Compare and contrast the two items below. List three ways the two items are alike. Then list three ways they are different. One similarity is listed to get you started. You can check your answers at the end of the lesson.

Item A: movies
Item B: live theater

Comparisons (similarities)

1. Both provide entertainment
2. _____
3. _____

Contrasts (differences)

1. _____
2. _____
3. _____

107

STRUCTURE

▶ Cause and Effect

A **cause** is something that takes place that makes something else happen. On the other hand, an **effect** is what happens *after* something takes place. Many reading passages incorporate cause and effect. For example, a passage could explain the *cause* for increased electricity costs and the *effect* these rising costs have on small businesses. A passage may also be limited to discussing only a cause (for example, increased electricity costs) or only an effect (small businesses struggle to pay high electricity bills). It all depends on the writer's choice. However, certain things are standard in a cause and effect passage. Keep reading to learn more.

Transitions for Cause and Effect

Just as certain transitions tell readers whether two things are similar or different, or in what order events occur, other words tell readers whether things are causes or effects. Watch for these transitions as you read.

WORDS THAT SHOW CAUSE	
because (of)	created (by)
since	caused (by)

WORDS THAT SHOW EFFECT		
since	therefore	hence
so	consequently	as a result

Opinions about Cause and Effect

Sometimes, writers offer their opinions about why something happened (cause). Or they might explain what they think will happen because of a certain event (effect). As a reader, you need to consider how reasonable those opinions are. Are the writer's ideas logical? Does the writer support the conclusions offered?

As a reader you will also have to decide which opinions make more sense to you. Is the cause likely to have that result? Does the author's argument make sense?

▶ Practice 4

Following are two paragraphs. They consider how a no-smoking policy would affect an office. Read them carefully. Then answer the questions that follow. You can check your answers at the end of the lesson.

Paragraph A

A no-smoking policy would be disastrous. Over one-third of our employees smoke half a pack a day. If they can't smoke in the office, they will have to leave the building. As a result, they will have to take longer breaks. This will interrupt their work. They will also have to take fewer breaks. And their breaks will be farther apart. This means longer stretches of time between cigarettes. Hence, many of these employees will be irritable. This irritability will surely affect their coworkers. Furthermore, long-time smokers may quit work, rather than adhere to this strict policy.

Paragraph B

A no-smoking policy would be a great benefit to all of us. We would be able to breathe smoke-free air. Furthermore, cigarette odor and smoke would no longer bother sensitive clients. In addition, smokers may find it easier to quit since they can't smoke as often during the day. Finally we will be able to cut the cost of healthcare coverage due to cigarette-related health problems and save employees money.

1. What effects does Paragraph A say the no-smoking policy will have? _____

STRUCTURE

2. What effects does Paragraph B say the no-smoking policy will have? _____
_____

3. What passage do you think sounds most reasonable? Why? _____
_____

By now, you should have a good idea about the way writers organize their ideas. This new understanding should help you to determine more easily what a passage is conveying. Use what you have learned in this lesson to answer the following questions. Don't forget to use skills you learned in Lesson 8 also.

▶ Review Practice

Read the following passage carefully and actively. Don't look up any unfamiliar words yet. First, try to decipher their meaning from context. Then answer the questions that follow.

> There are many fatal mistakes businesses can make. The Right Stuff was a toy store. It sold stuffed animals. It closed after it made a promise it couldn't keep. The Right Stuff had only been open a few weeks. It ordered a large shipment of Wilbur, the popular stuffed dog. Then The Right Stuff ran an ad in the newspaper. The ad claimed that The Right Stuff had Wilbur in-stock and on-sale starting Sunday.
>
> But by Friday, the Wilburs hadn't arrived. The Right Stuff called the warehouse. They learned the toys were on back order. They wouldn't even ship until the next Thursday. What could The Right Stuff do? On Sunday, employees had to tell customers that there were no Wilbur dolls. They offered I.O.U. coupons, but customers were mad. The sale was supposed to boost the store's business. Instead, it was a disaster. Two months later, The Right Stuff permanently closed its doors.

1. Which two organizing strategies does this writer use?
   a. time order
   b. order of importance
   c. compare and contrast
   d. cause and effect

2. *Fatal* means
   a. big.
   b. ruinous.
   c. obvious.
   d. minor.

3. What started the trouble for The Right Stuff? _____
_____

4. What is the main idea of this paragraph? _____
_____

Check your answers to see how you did. Could you see how each cause led to an effect? Could you see how each effect then caused another effect?

▶ Answers

Practice 1

There are several ways to fill in the blanks. One option is below. Notice how much more fluid the paragraph is with transitions.

> Yesterday, I went to work early to get some extra filing done. As soon as I got there, the phone started ringing. A moment later, my boss walked in. Right away he asked me to type a letter. Then, he asked me to set up a conference call. When I looked at my watch, it was already 11:00.

Practice 2

There are many ways to organize these ideas. Here is one example:

Order of Importance

1. You will develop a better understanding of yourself and others.
2. You will learn new information and ideas.
3. You will improve your reading comprehension.
4. You will broaden your vocabulary.
5. You will increase your reading speed.

Order of Presentation

1. You will develop a better understanding of yourself and others.
2. You will learn new information and ideas.
3. You will improve your reading comprehension.
4. You will broaden your vocabulary.
5. You will increase your reading speed.

The way your paragraph turns out depends on how you decided to order the ideas. The following are two sample paragraphs ordered from most to least important and from least to most important. The main idea is stated in the first sentence in each paragraph. The topic sentence is in boldface type and the transitions are underlined.

Most to Least Important

There are many benefits to reading more often. <u>First and foremost,</u> reading more will give you a better understanding of yourself and others. You will <u>also</u> learn new information and ideas. <u>Furthermore,</u> you will improve your reading comprehension. You will begin to understand more of what you read. <u>In addition,</u> you will increase both your vocabulary and your reading speed.

Least to Most Important

There are many benefits to reading more often. <u>First of all,</u> by reading more, you will increase your reading speed. You will be able to read more in less time. <u>Second,</u> you will broaden your vocabulary. <u>Third,</u> you will improve your reading comprehension. You will understand more of what you read. <u>Furthermore,</u> you will learn new information and ideas. <u>Most importantly,</u> you will develop a better understanding of yourself and others.

Practice 3

Answers will vary. Here is one possibility.

Comparisons (similarities)

1. Both provide entertainment.
2. Both use actors.
3. Both can be comedy or drama.

Contrasts (differences)

1. Movies are prerecorded; theater is live.
2. Movies require electricity to be displayed; theater does not necessarily require electricity.
3. Movies can be shown several times per a day, while live theater is performed usually only once or twice per day.

Practice 4

1. Paragraph A says that the no-smoking policy will have the following effects:
   - Smokers will take longer breaks. This will interrupt their work.
   - Smokers will have to take fewer breaks. This will make them irritable.
   - Smokers' irritability will affect their coworkers.
   - Long-time smokers may quit work.

STRUCTURE

2. Paragraph B says the no-smoking policy will have the following effects:
   - Everyone will be able to breathe smoke-free air.
   - Cigarette odor and smoke would no longer bother sensitive clients.
   - Healthcare coverage would cost less.
   - Employees will save money.
3. Answers will vary

Review Practice
1. The writer uses **a** and **d**—time order and cause and effect.
2. *Fatal* means bringing about misfortune, or *ruinous* (**b**). The main clue is that The Right Stuff closed down just two months after the incident.
3. The trouble was started by the ad. The first event in this chain reaction was ordering the Wilbur dogs, but that didn't cause the problem. The problem began with the ad. It said that the dogs were in stock.
4. The main idea of this paragraph is stated in the first sentence: "There are many fatal mistakes businesses can make." The rest of the passage gives a specific example of such mistakes.

CHAPTER

10 ▶ Language and Style

The language and style a writer uses gives readers even more clues about the text. Sometimes, the main idea won't be stated directly, and you will have to use these clues to understand what the author is trying to convey. This lesson will show how understanding the language and style of a paragraph can improve your reading comprehension skills.

▶ Point of View

Point of view is the person or position through which you see things. People can look at an object from many different points of view. You can look at it from above, below, behind, beside, and so on. How you see the object depends on your point of view. In writing, the point of view is like a filter. It's the voice through which the writer shares his or her ideas. What readers learn from a text depends on who is telling it to them. Thus, point of view is important in writing. Who will tell the readers the writer's ideas? Who will narrate the story?

LANGUAGE AND STYLE

Three Points of View

There are three points of view writers can use. They are the **first person**, **second person**, and **third person points of view**. A writer chooses the point of view depending upon the particular topic and purpose of the passage. The point of view helps a writer create a particular effect because each point of view works differently; each creates a different relationship between a reader and writer.

First-Person Point of View

The first-person point of view is a personal one. The writer uses the pronouns *I* or *we* and thus shares his or her own feelings, experiences, and ideas with readers.

Example:

I knew I was going to be late, but there was no way to get in touch with my boss.

This point of view creates a closeness between the reader and writer. By using the pronouns, *I, my, mine, we, our,* or *us,* the writer or narrator shares his feelings or ideas with the reader. The relationship between reader and writer is personal and creates a feeling of confidentiality because the writer is talking directly to the reader.

Second-Person Point of View

In the second-person point of view, writers use the pronoun *you*. The writer addresses the reader directly and makes the reader feel involved in the action.

Example:

You knew you were going to be late, but there was no way to get in touch with your boss.

The second-person point of view singles you (as the reader) out as an individual and makes you feel a part of what you are reading.

Third-Person Point of View

The third-person point of view offers readers the voice of an "outsider." There is no direct reference to the writer (first person, *I/we*) or the reader (second person, *you*). The writer uses the pronouns *he, she, it,* or *they*.

Example:

He knew he was going to be late. But there was no way to get in touch with his boss.

The third-person point of view creates a distance between the reader and the writer (or narrator). With the third-person point of view, there's no direct person-to-person contact (me to you). Rather, someone else is speaking to the reader.

▶ Practice 1

Change the point of view from third person to first person. Then check your answers at the end of the lesson.

1. They decided it would be best for them not to join the others.

2. The babysitter was annoyed by the last-minute cancellation.

3. People enjoy meals at nice restaurants.

Subjective versus Objective

The first person point of view is **subjective** (based on the thoughts, feelings, and experiences of the speaker or writer). However, ideas often carry more weight if they are **objective** (unaffected by the thoughts, feelings, and experiences of the speaker or writer). An objective person is outside of the action. He or she isn't personally involved; therefore, his or her ideas are likely to be more fair to everyone.

LANGUAGE AND STYLE

Example:

> **Subjective:** I don't like the biweekly pay period. Why should I have to wait two weeks to get paid?
>
> **Objective:** The biweekly pay period is a problem. It's unfair to make employees wait two weeks to get paid.

Most people would say that the second passage makes a better argument. The subjective passage doesn't sound like a thoughtful argument. Instead, it sounds like a complaint. The first-person, or subjective, point of view can create a wonderful closeness between writer and reader, but it's often less effective in an argument.

▶ Word Choice

You already know that being observant is an important part of reading. Writers make a lot of decisions. They decide what to say and how to say it. They choose to use particular points of view and particular words for a reason. Some authors choose to clearly state their ideas, but sometimes, they *suggest* their ideas instead. They don't explicitly state their ideas; rather they leave clues to tell the reader what the writer is saying. That's why it's important for readers to be observant.

Being observant means looking closely at what you read, so you can see the writer's strategies. This will help you understand the text. You've already learned many of these strategies. For example, you know to look for the way writers arrange ideas. You also know to look for the point of view.

It's also helpful to look for:

- particular words phrases the writer uses
- how those words and phrases are arranged in sentences
- word patterns or sentence patterns that are repeated
- important details about people, places, and things

The Importance of Word Choice

Even words that mean almost the same thing can make a different impression on a reader. For example, look at *slim* and *thin*. If you say your aunt is thin, that means one thing. If you say she is slim, that means something else. Slim has a different **connotation** (a word's suggested meaning) than thin. It's not **denotation** (how the word is defined in a dictionary). It's about what the word makes you think or feel when you read it. Slim and thin have almost the same definition in the dictionary, but slim suggests more grace and class than thin. Slim is a positive word. It suggests that your aunt is healthy. Thin, however, does not. Thin also suggests that your aunt is too skinny. Thin and slim then have different connotations. Therefore, the words that authors choose to describe things can tell readers a lot.

Noticing word choice is especially important when the main idea of a reading passage isn't clear. For example, look at the following paragraph. It's a letter of recommendation. There's no topic sentence. Use your powers of observation to uncover the writer's message.

> This letter regards my former office assistant, Jane Rosenberg. Jane usually completed her work on time. She proofread it carefully. She is an able typist. She is familiar with several word processing programs. She also knows some legal terms and procedures, which was helpful. Jane was always on time. She always asked if she had a question.

Think about what message this letter sends to its reader:

- **A.** Jane Rosenberg is a great office assistant. Hire her right away!
- **B.** Jane Rosenberg is an average employee. She doesn't do outstanding work, but she's capable and reliable.
- **C.** Jane Rosenberg is a bad worker. Don't even think about hiring her.

LANGUAGE AND STYLE

Clearly, the writer does not think that Jane is an outstanding employee. Nor is she saying that Jane is a bad employee. The words she uses suggest that Jane is average. How can you come to this conclusion? By looking carefully at the words the writer has chosen, you can understand the writer's message.

OBSERVATION	CONCLUSION
The first sentence is neutral. The writer doesn't say, "I'm happy to recommend" or "my wonderful office assistant." The sentence is flat, without emotion.	The writer doesn't feel strongly about Jane. She doesn't want to suggest that Jane is a great employee. At the same time, she doesn't want to suggest that Jane would be a bad hire.
The writer uses "usually" in the second sentence.	Jane is good about meeting deadlines but not great. She may not always get work done on time.
The writer says that Jane proofreads her work carefully.	Jane makes sure she does quality work. She's not sloppy.
The writer calls Jane an "able" typist.	*Able* is a pretty neutral word; it suggests that Jane types well enough, but that she could do a lot better. She's probably not a very fast typist.
The writer says that Jane is "familiar with" several word processing programs.	Jane knows a little about the programs but isn't an expert. She can probably do a few basic things in each program, but she would have trouble doing complex projects.
The writer says that Jane knows "some legal terms and procedures."	Jane's knowledge of legal terms and procedures is limited. She knows a little, but not a lot. She's better than someone who knows nothing, but she's no expert.
The writer says Jane "was always on time."	Jane is a reliable employee.
The writer says that Jane "always asked if she had a question."	Jane won't assume things. If she's unsure, she'll ask because she wants to be sure she has it right.

▶ Practice 2

Now it's your turn. Following is another letter about Jane. Read the letter carefully. Then, fill in the chart on the next page. What do you see? What can you conclude from what you notice? Once you fill in the chart, answer the question that follows. When you are done, check your answers at the end of the lesson.

I am pleased to recommend my former office assistant, Jane Rosenberg. I could always count on Jane to get her work done on time. I also knew she would proofread it very carefully. In addition, she is an outstanding typist and has also mastered several word processing programs. Furthermore, she knows legal terms and procedures inside and out. That was a tremendous help. I could always count on Jane to be on time, and I knew she would check with me if she had any questions.

LANGUAGE AND STYLE

OBSERVATION	CONCLUSION

Look at your observations and conclusions. What message is this writer sending?

- **A.** Jane is a great office assistant. Hire her right away.
- **B.** Jane is an average employee. She doesn't do outstanding work, but she is capable and reliable.
- **C.** Jane is a bad worker. Don't even think about hiring her.

▶ Style

Understanding **style** is important to reading success. Writers use different structures to organize their ideas. They also use different styles to express those ideas. Being aware of style helps you see what writers are trying to convey.

Style is also important for another reason. It's often what makes readers like or dislike certain writers or types of writing. You may not change your taste after this lesson, but you will probably be able to appreciate and understand many different kinds of writers and styles. Style consists of three elements:

- sentence structure
- level of detail and description
- level of formality

Sentence Structure

Sentences can vary greatly. They can be short and simple. They can also be long and complex, with lots of ideas packed together. Writers can use mostly one kind of sentence, or they can use a variety of sentence sizes, known as **sentence structure**. Sometimes sentences will all sound the same. Other times sentences will vary in word order and structure.

Level of Detail and Description

The level of description and detail has a large effect on the reader. Some writers are quite descriptive. Others offer only a few details. Here are two things to consider:

1. How specific is the writer? Does he write, "dog" (general) or "Labrador retriever" (specific)? Does she write "some" (general) or "three and a half pounds" (specific)?
2. How much description does the writer provide? Does he write, "Mr. Zee is my manager" (non-descriptive)? Or does he offer some description: "Mr. Zee, my manager, is a tall man with piercing eyes and a mustache"? Or does he go even further: "Mr. Zee, my manager, is six-foot-ten with eyes that pierce like knives and a mustache like Charlie Chaplin" (very descriptive)?

Notice the increasing level of detail in the following examples. The first sentence is very general. The second sentence adds some detail. The third sentence gets even more specific.

1. Charles is a bank teller.
2. Charles is a bank teller at Pennview Savings.
3. Charles is a bank teller at Pennview Savings, the first bank in this city.

1. Let's meet after work on the corner.
2. Let's meet after work on the corner of 58th and Broadway.
3. Let's meet at 6:15 P.M., on the corner of 58th and Broadway.

▶ Practice 3

Change the style of the following sentences. Add specific description and detail. When you are done, check your answers at the end of the lesson.

1. He ate a huge breakfast this morning.
   Descriptive Version:
   _____
   _____
   _____
   _____

2. Please dress up for the party.
   Descriptive Version:
   _____
   _____
   _____
   _____

3. The new gym has lots of equipment.
   Descriptive Version:
   _____
   _____
   _____
   _____

LANGUAGE AND STYLE

Level of Formality

Writers must decide how **formal** or **informal** they should be when they write. They decide the level of formality based on their audience and their purpose.

Writers can use slang (which is informal), proper language, or anything in between. They can address readers by their first names (casual) or by their title (formal). For example, the following sentences use two different levels of formality.

Let's get together after work on Thursday.

We invite you to join us for a social gathering at the close of business on Thursday.

Notice the drastic difference in style. The first sentence, likely directed at a friend, is casual and informal. The second sentence, on the other hand, is formal. Yet, both sentences send the same message; they just do it in different styles.

▶ Practice 4

Rank the following sentences from 1 to 3 (1 is the most formal and 3 is the least formal). When you are done, check your answers at the end of the lesson.

1. ____ Sales have improved.
   ____ These figures show that sales have increased.
   ____ Sales are up!

2. ____ You're doing great work, O'Brien.
   ____ Nice job, O'Brien.
   ____ Your performance is above our expectations, O'Brien.

So far you have learned that style is one thing writers use to express their ideas. Style consists of three elements: sentence structure, level of description and detail, and level of formality. Some writers use a very formal style while others are more casual. Remember, style depends on the writer's audience and purpose.

▶ Review Practice

Read the following passage carefully and answer the questions that follow. When you are done, check your answers at the end of the lesson.

Our company plans to merge with A+ systems, but the merger will have dire consequences for employees. First, the merger will force many of us to relocate. Second, many of us will be transferred to new departments. But most importantly, a merger means that hundreds of us will lose our jobs.

1. Which sentence states the main idea of this passage?
   a. The merger would be great for the company.
   b. The merger wouldn't change things too much.
   c. The merger would be bad for employees.
   d. The merger will benefit employees.

2. Which structure does this writer use to organize his ideas?
   a. time order
   b. cause and effect
   c. order of importance
   d. both **b** and **c**

3. Which point of view does the writer use in this passage?
   a. first person
   b. second person
   c. third person
   d. fourth person

LANGUAGE AND STYLE

4. Based on the point of view, you can conclude that the writer is
   a. an employer.
   b. an employee.
   c. an outside consultant.
   d. a business journalist.

5. The word *dire* means
   a. minimal.
   b. expected.
   c. disastrous.
   d. tranquil.

6. How would you describe the writer's tone or message?
   a. objective
   b. positive
   c. subjective
   d. indifferent

You should be able to apply what you have learned to all that you read. Now you know how authors write—you see how the words they use, the point of view from which they write, and the types of sentences they choose influence your understanding of a passage. You also understand how authors use style to create meaning.

▶ Answers

Practice 1

The changed pronouns are italicized below.

1. *I/We* decided it would be best for *me/us* not to join the others.
2. *I* was annoyed by the last-minute cancellation.
3. *I/We* enjoy meals at nice restaurants.

Practice 2

1.

OBSERVATION	CONCLUSION
The first sentence is positive. The writer "is pleased" to recommend Jane.	The writer was happy with Jane's work.
The writer says she could "always" count on Jane to get work done "on time."	Jane is a dependable worker. She meets deadlines.
The writer says she "knew" Jane would proofread "carefully."	Jane is always careful about her work.
She calls Jane an "outstanding" typist.	Jane types quickly and correctly.
She says that Jane has "mastered" several word processing programs.	Jane knows those programs inside and out. She can create all kinds of documents with them.
She says that Jane knows legal terms and procedures "inside and out."	Jane really knows legal terms and procedures.
The writer "could always count on Jane" to be on time.	Jane is never late.

2. a. Based on the high praise that Jane received, she will most likely be a great employee.

LANGUAGE AND STYLE

Practice 3
Answers will vary. Here are some examples.

1. Cedric ate two scrambled eggs, three slices of bacon, and four pieces of buttered toast for breakfast this morning.
2. Please wear an evening gown or tuxedo for Thursday's holiday party.
3. The brand new gym has seven Stairmasters, twenty stationary bikes, twenty-five treadmills, three sets of Nautilus equipment, four racquetball courts, and an Olympic-sized pool.

Practice 4
1. 2, 1, 3
2. 2, 3, 1

Review Practice
1. **c.** The first sentence in the passage is the topic sentence. It states that the merger will be bad for employees. The other sentences in the paragraph support that idea.
2. **d.** The writer describes the effects of the merger (which is the cause) on the employees. She lists these effects in order of importance. She saves the most important effect for last.
3. **a.** The writer uses the first-person pronouns *our*, *us*, and *we*. Also, there is no such thing as a fourth-person point of view.
4. **b.** The writer uses the first-person point of view. Thus, you can conclude that the author is an employee.
5. **c.** The consequences are all serious. They are all very negative. Thus, dire can't mean *minimal*. These effects may be *expected* (**b**), but the focus of the paragraph is the negative results.
6. **c.** The first-person point of view is based on the feelings and opinions of the narrator. Personal experiences are subjective.

CHAPTER 11 ▶ Drawing Conclusions

So far, you have studied how writers use structure and language to convey meaning to readers. Now it's time to put your new knowledge to work. In this lesson, you will look at passages that don't have a clear main idea. You will have to look carefully for clues. Then you can read between the lines to see what the author means.

▶ Finding an Implied Main Idea

When the main idea is **implied** (hinted at), there is not necessarily any topic sentence, so finding the main idea can be a challenge. But, you already know about the importance of word choice and style. You know how to look carefully at the text to find clues that will help you figure out the main idea.

To find an implied main idea, you have to find an idea that is general enough to cover the whole paragraph. Choices that are too specific and do not include all of the ideas in the paragraph obviously cannot be the main idea of the paragraph. You must ask yourself which idea is supported by all of the sentences in the paragraph. You also need to look for words and phrases that point to this main idea.

DRAWING CONCLUSIONS

Practice Passage 1
Read the following paragraph actively. Look for clues that suggest the main idea. Pay close attention to language. Notice how the writer describes Mr. Wilson. Then answer the questions that follow. Check your answers at the end of the lesson.

> At 9:00 every morning, my boss, Mr. Wilson, invades the office. He marches straight to my desk and demands his reports. He spends the day looking over my shoulder and barking orders. And he blames every mistake—even if it's *his* fault—on me.

1. Which sentence states the main idea of the passage?
   a. It's a pleasure to work for Mr. Wilson.
   b. Mr. Wilson is a good manager.
   c. Mr. Wilson is bossy and unfair.
   d. Mr. Wilson is always on time.

2. How did you figure out the main idea? List some of the clues you found.
   _____
   _____
   _____
   _____
   _____

There are a lot of clues in this practice passage. They probably helped you determine the implied main idea. Perhaps you also noticed something else while studying the passage. What point of view does the writer use? She uses the first person. Her description is based on her personal experience and feelings. Thus, her view is subjective. An outsider might have a different opinion of Mr. Wilson.

▶ Inference

Inferences are conclusions that we draw based on the clues the writer has given us. When you draw inferences, you must look for the clues (word choice, details, and so on) that suggest a certain conclusion, attitude, or point of view. You have to read between the lines in order to make a judgment about what an author was implying in the passage.

Questions that ask you about the meaning of a vocabulary word in the passage and those that ask what the passage suggests or implies are different from detail or main idea questions. Inference questions can be the most difficult to answer because they require you to draw meaning from the text when that meaning is implied rather than directly stated.

A good way to test whether you have drawn an acceptable inference is to ask yourself what evidence you have to support your conclusion. If you can't find any, you probably have the wrong answer. You need to be sure that your inference is logical and based on something suggested or implied in the passage—not by an opinion that you, or others, hold. You need to base your conclusions on evidence—facts, details, and other information—not on random guesses.

Practice Passage 2
A good way to solidify what you have learned about reading comprehension questions is for you to write similar test questions. After reading the passage on the next page, write one question for each of the following four question types that you will find on the Paragraph Comprehension portion of the ASVAB: fact or detail, main idea, inference, and vocabulary.

DRAWING CONCLUSIONS

For or Against?—That Is the Question

Andy is the most unreasonable, pigheaded, subhuman life-form in the entire galaxy, and he makes me so angry I could scream! Of course, I love him like a brother. I sort of have to because he is my brother. More than that, he's my twin! That's right. Andy and Amy (that's me) have the same curly hair and dark eyes and equally stubborn temperaments. Though we may look alike, we usually take diametrically opposite positions on most issues. If I say, "day," you can count on Andy to say, "night."

Just this week, the big buzz in school was all about the PTA's proposal to adopt a school dress code. Every student would be required to wear a uniform. Uniforms! Can you imagine? Oh, they won't be military-style uniforms, but the clothes would be uniform in color. The dress style would be sort of loose and liberal.

Boys would wear white or blue button-down shirts, a school tie, blue or gray pants, and a navy blue blazer or cardigan sweater. Girls would wear white or blue blouses or sweaters, blue or gray pants or skirts, along with a navy blue blazer or cardigan sweater. Socks or tights could be black, gray, blue, or white. The teachers are divided: Some are in favor of the uniforms, others are opposed. The principal has asked the students to express their opinion by voting on the issue before the final is made decision. The principal has the final word on the dress code.

I think a dress code is a good idea. The reason is simple. School is tough enough without worrying about looking cool every single day. The fact is, the less I have to decide in the morning, the better. I can't tell you how many mornings I look into my closet and just stare, unable to decide what to wear. Of course, there are other mornings when my room looks like a cyclone had hit it, with bits and pieces of a dozen different possible outfits on the bed, on the floor, or dangling from the lamps. I also wouldn't mind not seeing guys with oversized jeans and shirts so huge they would fit a sumo wrestler. And, I certainly would welcome not seeing kids showing off designer-labeled clothes.

Andy is appalled at my opinion. He says he can't believe that I would be willing to give up my all-American teenage birthright by dressing like—well, like a typical teenager. "Kurt Cobain never wore a school uniform. Jay-Z wouldn't have been caught dead in a school uniform!" he declared. Andy was now on his soapbox. "When I am feeling political, I want to be able to wear clothes made of natural, undyed fibers, sewn or assembled in countries that do not pollute the environment or exploit child labor. If I have to wear a uniform, I won't feel like me!"

To which I replied, "So your personal heroes didn't wear school uniforms. Big deal! They went to high school about a million years ago! I feel sorry for you, brother dear. I had no idea that your ego is so fragile that it would be completely destroyed by gray or blue pants, a white or blue shirt, a tie, and a blazer."

That really made him angry. Then he said, "You're just mimicking what you hear that new music teacher saying."

"Is that so? Anyone who doesn't agree with you is automatically stupid. And that's the stupidest thing of all!" I said.

Fortunately, the bell rang ending the argument, and we went (thankfully) to our separate classes.

The vote for or against uniforms took place later that day. The results of the vote and the principal's decision will be announced next week. I wonder what it will be? I know how I voted, and I'm pretty sure I know how Andy voted.

How would you vote—for or against?

Questions

1. Detail Question: _____
_____

a. _____
b. _____
c. _____
d. _____

2. Main Idea Question: _____
_____

a. _____
b. _____
c. _____
d. _____

3. Inference Question: _____
_____

a. _____
b. _____
c. _____
d. _____

4. Vocabulary question: _____
_____

a. _____
b. _____
c. _____
d. _____

▶ Implied Information

Often writers have thoughts that they don't want to say directly. So, they use **suggestion** to get their ideas across. They suggest things in many ways. Some clues are action clues—what people said and did. Clues can also come in the form of details, word choice, and style. For example, look at the following passage.

Dennis was scared. His knees were weak. He looked down. The water was twenty feet below. He looked up again, quickly. He tried to think of something else. He tried to reassure himself. "It's only twenty feet!" he said aloud. But that only made it sound worse. Twenty feet! He felt dizzy and hot.

The writer could have said, "Dennis was scared. He was afraid of heights." Instead the writer *suggests* this information cause. The author *shows* you how Dennis feels. You see what he thinks and feels. Through these details, you can conclude that he is afraid of heights. The repetition of "twenty feet" is another clue, so is the sentence structure. Notice that the sentences are short and choppy. In fact, they sound a little panicky. This helps show how Dennis felt.

Practice Passage 3

Here is an excerpt from a short story. Read the passage carefully. Then answer the questions that follow.

Anne tensed when she heard the front door open. She waited in the kitchen near the dirty dishes in the sink. She knew her neat-freak roommate, Chandra, would look there first. Taking a deep breath, Anne thought about what she would say to her. She waited.

A moment later, Chandra stepped into the kitchen. Her face dropped immediately when she saw the dishes piled high in the sink. Pointing angrily at them, Chandra asked, "What are those filthy things still doing in the sink?"

"Uh, I haven't gotten to them yet," Anne replied. She tried to remain calm.

Chandra yelled, "How many times have I told you that I like to have my house clean at all times?"

"Well, you say that every time I leave any kind of mess, no matter how small. You have to understand that I have an important exam this week and can't spend all my free time cleaning," Anne replied.

"Then you should hire a maid to do it for you!" shouted Chandra.

DRAWING CONCLUSIONS

Anne could only walk out of the room in response. She knew Chandra was not the perfect roommate, but right now, Anne was more worried about her exam.

1. Why does Chandra get mad?
   a. because Anne didn't greet her at the door
   b. because she had a bad day
   c. because Anne didn't do the dishes
   d. because Anne is lazy

2. Why didn't Anne do the dishes?
   a. because she just returned home
   b. because she wanted to start a fight
   c. because she isn't a maid
   d. because she had to study

3. Why is Anne upset with Chandra?
   a. because Chandra pays less rent than Anne
   b. because Chandra wants to hire a maid
   c. because Chandra never cleans up
   d. because Chandra expects Anne to clean up even small messes immediately

Writers often suggest ideas and other information. You have to read between the lines to identify them. Look for clues in the action. What do people say and do? Look for more clues in details, word choice, and style. Use your sense of logic to answer questions and think about what the clues mean.

Review Practice
Read the passage and answer the questions. Then check your answers at the end of the lesson.

Dealing with irritable patients is a great challenge for healthcare workers. It is critical that you do not lose your patience when confronted by such a patient. When handling irate patients, remember that they are not angry with you; they are simply projecting their anger at something else onto you. If you respond to these patients as irritably as they act with you, you will only increase their hostility, making it much more difficult to give them proper treatment. The best thing to do is to remain calm, and ignore any imprecations patients may hurl your way. Such patients may be irrational and may not realize what they are saying. Often, these patients will purposely try to anger you to get some reaction out of you. If you react to this behavior with anger, they win by getting your attention, but you both lose because the patient is less likely to get proper care.

1. The word *irate* as it is used in the passage most nearly means
   a. irregular.
   b. cheerful.
   c. ill tempered.
   d. lazy.

2. The passage suggests that healthcare workers
   a. easily lose control of their emotions.
   b. are better off not talking to their patients.
   c. must be careful when dealing with irate patients because the patients may sue the hospital.
   d. may provide inadequate treatment if they become angry at patients.

3. An *imprecation* is most likely
   a. an object.
   b. a curse.
   c. a joke.
   d. a medication.

4. Which of the following best expresses the writer's views about irate patients?
   a. Some irate patients just want attention.
   b. Irate patients are always miserable.
   c. Irate patients should be made to wait for treatment.
   d. Managing irate patients is the key to a successful career.

DRAWING CONCLUSIONS

By now, you should know what you need to pass the Paragraph Comprehension subtest. If you still want more practice, try these additional resources:

- *Reading Comprehension Success in 20 Minutes a Day*, 3rd Ed. (LearningExpress)
- *501 Reading Comprehension Questions*, 3rd Ed. (LearningExpress)

▶ Answers

Practice 1

1. **c.** The main idea is that Mr. Wilson is bossy and unfair.
2. There are lots of clues in the passage. First, the writer uses the word "invades." This word suggests that Mr. Wilson is trying to take over something that isn't his. It suggests that he isn't wanted. Second, Mr. Wilson spends the day "barking orders." He doesn't ask. He doesn't consider feelings. He just demands that things get done. Furthermore, the last sentence shows you that Wilson is unfair—*his* mistakes get blamed on someone else.

Practice 2

Here is one question of each type based on the passage. Your questions may be different, but these will give you an idea of the kinds of questions that could be asked.

1. Detail question: Amy and Andy fight because
   a. neither one is able to convince the other to change his or her point of view.
   b. they are twins.
   c. they always take the opposite view on issues.
   d. they don't like each other.

2. Main idea question: Which of the following is the best statement of Andy's position on the issue presented in the story?
   a. School clothing should reflect parents' values.
   b. Wearing school uniforms means one less decision every morning.
   c. How one dresses should be an expression of one's personality.
   d. Teenagers should never follow the latest fashion trends.

3. Inference question: Amy's position on school uniforms is most likely based on
   a. logical conclusions drawn from her own observation and personal experience.
   b. an emotional response to what she has been told by people in authority.
   c. her preference for designer-labeled clothes.
   d. not liking anything her brother likes.

4. Vocabulary question: Read the following sentences from the story:

   Andy is <u>appalled at</u> my opinion. He says he can't believe that I would be willing to give up my all-American teenage birthright by dressing like—well, like a typical teenager.

   As it is used in these sentences, what does *appalled at* mean?
   a. angry
   b. in denial
   c. supportive of
   d. horrified by

DRAWING CONCLUSIONS

Practice 3
1. **c.** Chandra is a neat freak and expects Anne to clean up messes immediately, even if Anne is preparing for an important exam.
2. **d.** Anne says that she has an important exam this week, which implies that she has to study. The other choices are not implied in the story.
3. **d.** Anne is upset because Chandra is not reasonable in her expectations of cleanliness. Chandra expects Anne to keep the apartment spotless no matter what.

Review Practice
1. **c.** This is a vocabulary question. Irate means *ill-tempered*. It should be clear that choice **b**, *cheerful*, is not the answer; dealing with happy patients is normally not "a great challenge." Patients that are choice **a**, *irregular*, or choice **d**, *lazy*, may be a challenge in their own way, but they aren't likely to rouse healthcare workers to anger. In addition, the passage explains that irate patients are not "angry at you," and irate is used as a synonym for *irritable*, which describes the patients in the first sentence.
2. **d.** This is an inference question, as the phrase "the passage suggests" might have told you. The idea that angry healthcare workers might give inadequate treatment is implied by the passage as a whole, which seems to be an attempt to prevent angry reactions to irate patients. Furthermore, the last sentence in particular makes this inference possible: "If you react to this behavior with anger . . . you both lose because the patient is less likely to get proper care." Choice **c** is not correct, because while it may be true that some irate patients have sued hospitals in the past, there is no mention of lawsuits anywhere in this passage. Likewise, choice **b** is incorrect; the passage does suggest ignoring patients' insults, but it does not recommend not talking to patients—it simply recommends not talking angrily. And while it may be true that some healthcare workers may lose control of their emotions, the passage does not provide any facts or details to support choice **a**, that they "easily lose control." Watch out for key words like *easily* that may distort the meaning of the passage.
3. **b.** If you didn't know what an imprecation is, the context should reveal that it's something you can ignore, so neither choice **a**, an *object*, nor choice **d**, a *medication*, is a likely answer. Furthermore, choice **c** is not likely either, since an irate patient is not likely to be making jokes.
4. **a.** The writer seems to believe that some irate patients just want attention, as is suggested when the writer says, "Often these patients will purposely try to anger you to get some reaction out of you. If you react to this behavior with anger, they win by getting your attention." It should be clear that choice **b** cannot be the answer because it includes an absolute: "Irate patients are always miserable." Perhaps some of the patients are often miserable, but an absolute like *always* is wrong. Besides, this passage refers to patients who may be irate in the hospital, but we have no indication of what these patients are like at other times, and miserable and irate are not exactly the same thing. Choice **c** is also incorrect because the purpose of the passage is to ensure that patients receive "proper treatment" and that irate patients are not discriminated against because of their behavior. Thus, "irate patients should be made to wait for treatment" is not a logical answer. Finally, choice **d** cannot be correct because, although it may be true, there is no discussion of career advancement in the passage.

SECTION

Vocabulary for the Word Knowledge Subtest

Effective communication skills—including vocabulary and spelling—are essential to everything you do. A good vocabulary increases your ability to understand reading material and express yourself in both speaking and writing. Without a broad vocabulary, your ability to learn is limited. The good news is that vocabulary skills can be developed with practice.

The Word Knowledge portion of the ASVAB is basically a vocabulary test. Combined with the Paragraph Comprehension score, Word Knowledge helps make up your Verbal Equivalent score—it's one of the all-important subtests that determine whether you will be allowed to enlist. Your ability to understand your training materials depends in part on your reading comprehension and vocabulary skills

There are two different kinds of questions on the Word Knowledge subtest:

- **Synonyms:** Identifying words that mean the same as the given words.
- **Context:** Determining the meaning of a word or phrase by noting how it is used in a sentence or paragraph.

You already have had some practice identifying the meanings of words by examining their context in Section 3: Reading Comprehension for the Paragraph Comprehension subtest. You will get some more practice in this section, and you will also learn about synonyms and word parts, including word roots, prefixes, and suffixes. These lessons will help you improve and develop your vocabulary skills, teaching you how to break down words into parts you recognize so that you can decipher their meanings. Remember, you are not penalized for guessing on the ASVAB, so these methods will help you improve your guessing power when you encounter unknown words on the Word Knowledge subtest.

There are three ways we learn vocabulary:

- from the **sound** of words
- from the **structure** of words
- from the **context**; how the word is used

Learning words is therefore a three-step process.

1. Ask yourself, "Does this word **sound** like anything I've ever heard?"

If not, ask

2. "Does any part of the word **look** familiar?"

If not, then ask

3. "How is this word **used** in the sentence I read or heard?"

Try asking yourself this sequence of questions with each unfamiliar word you encounter. As you learn more about how vocabulary works, you will find that you already know some of the words, and you can use your new knowledge to figure out the others.

CHAPTER 12 ▶ Word Parts

The value of learning word parts is that they act as a kind of access key that gives you clues about other words in the same family as the word you know. **Roots**, **prefixes**, and **suffixes** are word elements that share characteristics.

English words share so many traits because they descend from a long line of intermingled Indo-European languages. Many English words come from Greek and Latin. Again, the point of learning to recognize word parts is that they give you access to whole groups of words when you know a few language families.

The best way to improve your vocabulary is to learn word parts. Using word parts to increase vocabulary works in two ways:

1. You may already know a given root, prefix, or suffix that can guide you in determining the meaning of an unfamiliar word. For example, you may know that the root *hydro* suggests water. Therefore, if you came across the word *hydrotherapy*, you would figure it is a treatment that uses water.
2. If you don't know the part by itself, you may recognize it from a word you know. By association, then, you link the known meaning to that of an unfamiliar word. For example, you know that a fire hydrant stores water. Therefore, you associate the root *hydro* to water and deduce the meaning of *hydrotherapy*.

▶ Roots

Roots are the pieces of words that carry direct meaning. Generally roots of English words are derived from ancient Greek and Latin words. Because so many English words have their source in certain recurring root words, knowing some of the most commonly used roots gives you access to the meaning of many words at once. When you combine your knowledge of roots with your knowledge of **prefixes** and **suffixes**—the small parts of words that go at the beginning or end of words to change their meanings—you have the tools for deciphering the meanings of many words from their structure.

Definitions and Roots

The value of learning roots is that they give you clues about unfamiliar words that share the roots of words you do know.

Following are the definitions and roots of some words, along with other words that share their roots.

agoraphobic (*phobe* = fear): fear of open spaces
phobia, claustrophobia, xenophobia

antagonize (*agon* = struggle, contest): to struggle against
protagonist, agony, agonize

assimilate (*simul* = copy): to fit in
similar, simile, facsimile, simulate

attribute (*trib* = to give): a special quality
tributary, contribution, tribunal

audible (*aud* = hear): able to be heard
audition, audience, auditorium

belligerent (*bell* = war): warlike
bellicose, antebellum

benevolent (*ben* = good): kind
benefactor, beneficiary, benign, benediction

biodegradable (*bio* = life): able to be broken down by living things
bionic, biology, antibiotic

chronic (*chron* = time): occurring over time
chronological, chronometer, chronicle

conspicuous (*spic, spec* = see): highly visible
spectacle, spectator, inspection, introspection

contradiction (*contra* = against, *dict* = say): the act or state of disagreeing
contrary, contrast, dictate, dictionary, interdict, dictation

credence (*cred* = believe): belief, believability
creed, credulous, credit, incredible

demographic (*demo* = people): having to do with the measurement of populations
democracy, demagogue

evident (*vid* = see): obvious
video, evidence, visible, provident

fidelity (*fid* = faith): faithfulness
fiduciary, infidel, infidelity

fluctuate (*flux, flu* = to flow): to rise and fall
fluid, fluidity, superfluous, influx

gregarious (*greg* = crowd, herd): sociable
egregious

impediment (*ped, pod* = foot; ped also means child): a barrier or hindrance
pedestal, pedestrian, pediment

incisive (*cis* = to cut): penetrating, clear cut
incision, precise, scissors

incognito (*cog, gno* = to know): unrecognizable
diagnosis, recognize, cognition, cognitive

inducement (*duc* = to lead): leading to an action
induction, reduction, introduction, reduce

inference (*fer* = bear or carry): guess or surmise
transfer, refer, reference, interfere

interrogate (*rog* = to ask): to question
surrogate, derogatory, arrogant

loquacious (*loq* = speak): talkative
eloquent, soliloquy

mediocre (*med* = middle): of medium quality, neither good nor bad
median, intermediate, mediator

WORD PARTS

nominal (*nom, nym* = name): in name only
nominate, nomenclature, synonym, anonymous

pathos (*path* = feeling): feeling of sympathy or pity
pathetic, empathy, sympathy, apathy

philanthropy (*phil* = love): giving generously to worthy causes
philosophy, Philadelphia, bibliophile

precedent (*ced* = go): a prior ruling or experience
intercede, procedure, succeed

protracted (*tract* = draw, pull): dragged out
tractor, distracted, attraction, subtracted

recapitulate (*cap* = head): to review in detail
capital, caption, captain, decapitate

rejected (*ject* = to throw or send): sent back
subject, dejected, interjected, projectile

remittance (*mit, mis* = to send): to pay or send back
submit, commission, permission

sophisticated (*soph* = wisdom): having style or knowledge
sophomore, sophistry, philosopher

tangential (*tang, tac, tig* = touch): touching slightly
tangent, tactical, tactile, contiguous

tenacious (*ten* = hold): unwilling to let go, stubborn
tenacity, contain, tenable

urbane (*urb* = city): polished, sophisticated
urban, suburban, urbanite

verify (*ver* = truth): to establish as truth
verity, veritable, veracious, aver

vivacious (*viv* = life): lively in manner
vivid, vital

▶ Practice 1

Fill in the blanks with words from the previous list. Check your answers at the end of the lesson.

1. His remarks were _____ and cut right to the heart of the subject.

2. It doesn't pay to _____ the opinions of those who are in authority.

3. His _____ arose from his deep desire to help those less fortunate than himself.

4. The store demanded the _____ of the required payment to clear the debt.

5. One of her best _____ is her clear-eyed wisdom.

6. Over the years, people from many countries have come to _____ into American life.

7. Public works projects in the 1930s set a _____ for social legislation for the next 60 years.

8. After the game, the commentators continued to _____ the key plays for those who had been unable to watch it.

9. By wearing a wig and glasses, Shana believed she was going _____.

10. It was the principal's duty to _____ the students and find out who was responsible for the vandalism.

▶ Practice 2

Answer the following with words from the previous list. Check your answers at the end of the lesson.

1. Which word stems from a root that means *good*? _____

2. Which word stems from a root that relates to *hearing*? _____

3. Which word stems from a root that means *to cut* or *kill*? _____

4. Which word stems from a root that means to *bear* or *carry*? _____

5. Which word stems from a root than means a *fear*? _____

6. Which word stems from a root that means *crowd*? _____

7. Which word stems from a root that suggests *touching*? _____

8. Which word stems from a root that means *belief*? _____

9. Which word stems from a root that suggests *speaking*? _____

10. Which word stems from a root that means *see*? _____

▶ Prefixes

Prefixes are word parts at the beginning of a root word that change or add to the word's meaning in some way. They are often seen in different forms and may fundamentally change the meaning of a root word—making it an opposite, for example. Or, a prefix may only remotely suggest meaning. The point of working with prefixes is not to memorize a batch of disconnected word parts but to become familiar with the most common examples. Then you may be able to figure out how a word's meaning may have been affected by a prefix.

For example, the Latin root *vert* means to turn. Look at what happens when you add different prefixes in front of that root:

- *con* (with or together) + *vert* = convert (transform—think turn together)
  She wanted to **convert** the old barn into a studio.
- *di* (two) + *vert* = divert (turn aside)
  He wanted to **divert** attention from the spectacle.
- *ex* (out of, away from) + *vert* = extrovert (an outgoing individual)
  He was an **extrovert** who was the life of every party.
- *in* (opposite) + *vert* = invert (turn over)
  He **inverted** the saucer over the cup.
- *intro* (inside) + *vert* = introvert (an inwardly directed person)
  She was an **introvert** who generally shied away from company.
- *re* (back or again) + *vert* = revert (turn back)
  He **reverted** to speaking Spanish with his grandmother.

Definitions and Prefixes

Following are some words with their prefixes and meanings, as well as other words that use the prefix.

antecedents (*ante* = before): something that comes before, especially ancestors
antenatal, antebellum, anteroom

antipathy (*anti* = against): hatred, feelings against
antiwar, antibiotic, antidote

WORD PARTS

circumvent (*circum, circ* = around): to get around
circumscribe, circulate, circumference

consensus (*con* = with, together): agreement on a course of action
congress, convivial, congregate

controversy (*contr* = against): public dispute
contrast, contrary

decimate (*dec* = ten): to destroy or kill a large portion of something
decimal, decibel

demote (*de* = down, away from): to lower in grade or position
decline, deflate

disinterested (*dis* = not, opposite of): not having selfish interest in (not the same as uninterested)
disappointed, disabled, disqualified

euphemism (*eu* = good, well): a more pleasant term for something distasteful
euphonious, eugenic, eulogy

exorbitant (*ex* = out of, away from): excessive (literally, out of orbit)
exhume, extort, exhale, export

illegible (*il* = not, opposite): not readable
illegal, illegitimate, illicit

intermittent (*inter* = between): occurring from time to time, occasional
intermediate, interlude, intermission

malevolent (*mal* = bad): cruel, evil
malady, malefactor, malice, malignant

precursor (*pre* = before): a form that precedes a current model
premeditate, premature, prevent, preview

prognosis (*pro* = before): opinion about the future state of something
provide, professional, produce

retrospect (*retro* = back, again): hindsight
retroactive, retrograde

subordinate (*sub* = under): lower in rank
subterranean, substrate, subscription

synthesis (*syn, sym* = with or together): the combination of many things into one
synthetic, symphony, symbiotic

transcend (*trans* = across): to go beyond
transfer, transportation, transatlantic

trivial (*tri* = three): unimportant
tripod, triangle, triennial

Note that some words translate very neatly into their components:

- Antipathy literally means feelings against (*anti* = against, *path* = feelings).
- Retrospect literally means looking back (*retro* = back, *spect* = to look or see).

But beware, in some cases, the connection between the meaning of the prefix and the meaning of the word is much less obvious. For instance, the word *trivial* comes from the place where, in ancient times, the three main caravan routes met and people exchanged gossip and bits of information. Today we use trivial to refer to small items of information that are relatively unimportant.

▶ Practice 3

Complete each of the following sentences with a word from the previous list. Check your answers at the end of the lesson.

1. The manager threatened to _____ the clerk if he came late one more time.

2. The union leaders finally reached a(n) _____ over the salary package.

3. The Civil War _____ both the land and the population of the South.

WORD PARTS

4. Because the signature was _____, no one knew who wrote the letter.

5. The choice had to be made by a(n) _____ person who would not benefit from the outcome.

6. Using too many _____ to avoid distasteful subjects weakens our ability to express ourselves clearly.

7. The boy always found a way to _____ authority and get his own way.

8. The photography exhibition showed the _____ between images and color.

9. Many people focus on the _____ things in life and ignore the more important matters.

10. Every January, the president of the club offers her _____ on the coming year.

▶ Practice 4

Mark the following statements as true or false according to the meaning of the underlined word. Check your answers at the end of the lesson.

_____ 1. Most people would want to pay an <u>exorbitant</u> sum for a theater ticket.

_____ 2. An <u>intermittent</u> action does not happen once.

_____ 3. A <u>retrospective</u> exhibition shows only recent works by an artist.

_____ 4. A <u>disinterested</u> person is bored with her work.

_____ 5. To <u>circumvent</u> an issue is to address it directly.

_____ 6. A <u>malevolent</u> character in a movie is usually the hero.

_____ 7. One's children are one's <u>antecedents</u>.

_____ 8. The bicycle is a <u>precursor</u> to a motorcycle.

_____ 9. If you have <u>antipathy</u> toward someone, you have little or no feeling at all.

_____ 10. We use <u>euphemisms</u> when we want to soften the meaning of what we say.

▶ Suffixes

You may remember from elementary school English classes that words are divided into something called parts of speech—primarily nouns (people, places, and things), verbs (action or existence words), and adjectives and adverbs (words which describe other words). **Suffixes** are word endings that often change the word's part of speech.

Thus, adding a suffix often changes the function of the word in a sentence without fundamentally changing the word's meaning. You can think of a suffix as the hat a word wears for a particular job in the sentence.

For example, take the word *devote*, meaning to dedicate time to the care of someone or something. Suffixes change the way the word works in a sentence.

- As a **verb**, it appears as it is:
  I will *devote* my time to my family.
- As a **noun**, it takes the *-tion* suffix and becomes devotion:
  His *devotion* to his family was well known.
- As an **adjective** modifying a noun, it takes the *-ed* suffix:
  He is a *devoted* family man.
- As an **adverb** modifying a verb, it takes the *-ly* suffix:
  He *devotedly* served his family for many years.

138

WORD PARTS

The table that follows shows commonly used suffixes. They are divided into the parts of speech they suggest for the words. Other words that contain those suffixes are listed. In the last column, you can add at least one other word you already know that uses the same suffix.

SUFFIX	MEANING	EXAMPLES	YOUR EXAMPLE
Noun Endings			
-tion	act or state of	retraction, contraction	
-ment	quality of	deportment, impediment	
-ian	one who is or does, relating to	tactician, patrician	
-ist	one who	feminist, philanthropist	
-ism	state or doctrine of	barbarism, materialism	
-ity	state of being	futility, civility	
-ology	study of	biology, psychology	
-escence	state of	adolescence, convalescence	
-y, -ry	state of	mimicry, trickery	
Adjective Endings			
-able	capable of	perishable, flammable	
-ic	causing, making	nostalgic, fatalistic	
-ile	pertaining to	senile, servile	
-ious	having the quality of	religious, glorious	
-ive	having the nature of	sensitive, divisive	
-less	without	guileless, reckless	
Verb Endings			
-ize	to bring about	colonize, plagiarize	
-ate	to make	decimate, tolerate	
-ify	to make	beautify, electrify	

Definitions and Suffixes

Following are some words with their suffixes and meanings. The words contain boldfaced suffixes that identify the word's part of speech. As you look at the words, think about words you already know that contain the same suffix.

agrar**ian**: having to do with agriculture or farming
   The farmer loved his agrarian life.
bigot**ry**: narrow-minded intolerance
   We must guard against bigotry wherever it exists.

WORD PARTS

consumm**ate**: to make complete
> The deal was consummated after long negotiations.

cop**ious**: plentiful
> She received copious praise for her excellent work.

cryp**tic**: mysterious, hidden
> Her cryptic comment was unclear to everyone.

defer**ment**: delay
> He wanted a deferment on paying his student loans.

etym**ology**: study of word origins
> The scholar was an authority on the etymology of words.

furt**ive**: underhanded and sly
> He had a furtive manner.

laud**able**: praiseworthy
> He had laudable intentions to do good in his community.

muta**tion**: a change in form
> The scientist found a significant mutation in the gene.

obsol**escence**: the state of being outdated
> The new designs were already headed for obsolescence.

par**ity**: equality
> He wanted parity with the other employees.

pragmat**ism**: faith in the practical approach
> His pragmatism helped him run a successful business.

protagon**ist**: one who is the central figure in a drama
> The protagonist was played by a great actor.

provocat**ive**: inciting to action
> The actions of a few demonstrators were provocative.

puer**ile**: childish
> The father's actions were puerile; his five-year-old was more mature.

recti**fy**: to correct
> He wanted to rectify the misunderstanding.

relent**less**: unstoppable
> He was relentless in his search for knowledge.

satir**ize**: to use humor to expose folly in institutions or people
> Comedians like to satirize politicians.

vener**ate**: to respect or worship
> He venerated his parents and protected their interests.

▶ Practice 5

Mark the following statements as true or false according to the meanings of the underlined words. Check your answers at the end of the lesson.

_____ 1. A <u>deferment</u> allows immediate action.

_____ 2. The <u>protagonist</u> is usually the most important person in a play.

_____ 3. People <u>venerate</u> things they do not respect.

_____ 4. <u>Obsolescence</u> adds value to merchandise.

_____ 5. <u>Etymology</u> is the study of insect life.

_____ 6. A <u>mutation</u> can be a change of form.

_____ 7. A <u>relentless</u> search is over quickly.

_____ 8. If there is a <u>copious</u> amount of something, you are likely to run out of it quickly.

_____ 9. A <u>furtive</u> glance is sly and secretive.

_____ 10. <u>Agrarian</u> life is found in the city.

WORD PARTS

▶ Practice 6

Complete the following sentences. Check your answers at the end of the lesson.

1. If you venerate something, you _____.

2. If you request a deferment, you want _____.

3. If you want to rectify a situation, you must _____.

4. If you are a relentless person, you _____.

5. If your motives are laudable, they are _____.

6. If you satirize something, you _____.

7. If you behave in a puerile manner, you are _____.

8. If you behave in a furtive way, you are being _____.

9. If you want parity at work, you want _____.

10. If you consummate arrangements for a trip, you _____.

By now you should be familiar with many word parts, from roots, to prefixes, to suffixes. You have not only learned new words, but you have also learned how to identify unfamiliar words by identifying parts of the word that you already know.

▶ Answers

Practice 1
1. incisive
2. contradict
3. philanthropy
4. remittance
5. attributes
6. assimilate
7. precedent
8. recapitulate
9. incognito
10. interrogate

Practice 2
1. benevolent
2. audible
3. incisive
4. inference
5. agoraphobia
6. gregarious
7. tangential
8. credence
9. contradict
10. evident

Practice 3
1. demote
2. consensus
3. decimated
4. illegible
5. disinterested
6. euphemisms
7. circumvent
8. synthesis
9. trivial
10. prognosis

Practice 4
1. false
2. true
3. false

4. false
5. false
6. false
7. false
8. true
9. false
10. true

Practice 5
1. false
2. true
3. false
4. false
5. false
6. true
7. false
8. false
9. true
10. false

Practice 6
1. respect it
2. a postponement
3. correct it
4. don't give up
5. praiseworthy
6. make fun of it
7. childish
8. sly and sneaky
9. equal treatment
10. finalize them

CHAPTER 13 ▶ Words in Context

Since you have already learned about context in Lesson 8 of the Reading Comprehension section, this lesson is mostly practice questions similar to those on the ASVAB.

Remember, **context** is the surrounding text in which a word is used. Most people use context to help them determine the meaning of an unknown word. A vocabulary question that gives you a sentence around the vocabulary word is usually easier to answer than one with little or no context. The surrounding text can help you as you look for synonyms in the sentences.

The best way to take meaning from context is to look for key words in sentences or paragraphs that convey the meaning of the text. If nothing else, the context will give you a means to eliminate wrong answer choices that clearly don't fit. The process of elimination will often leave you with the correct answer.

WORDS IN CONTEXT

► Practice 1

Choose the word that best fills the blank in the following sentences. Check your answers at the end of the lesson.

1. The main _____ Jim had was too many parking tickets.
   a. disaster
   b. search
   c. request
   d. problem

2. While trying to _____ his pet iguana from a tree, Travis fell and broke his ankle.
   a. examine
   b. transfer
   c. rescue
   d. pardon

3. The brand new sports car cost a(n) _____ amount of money.
   a. considerate
   b. conscientious
   c. lucrative
   d. considerable

4. We knew nothing about Betty, because she was so _____.
   a. expressive
   b. secretive
   c. emotional
   d. artistic

5. We were tired when we reached the _____, but the spectacular view of the valley below was worth the hike.
   a. circumference
   b. summit
   c. fulcrum
   d. nadir

6. The _____ of not turning in your homework is after-school detention.
   a. reward
   b. denial
   c. consequence
   d. cause

7. His suit had a(n) _____ odor, as if it had been closed up for a long time in an old trunk.
   a. aged
   b. dried-up
   c. musty
   d. decrepit

8. Every day, he had to deal with crowds of noisy, demanding people, so he longed most of all for _____.
   a. solitude
   b. association
   c. loneliness
   d. irrelevancy

9. Julia was blamed for the town's bad fortune, and so she was _____ by everyone.
   a. regarded
   b. shunned
   c. neglected
   d. forewarned

10. When Tasia described the blackbird as black, the teacher reminded him that his description was _____.
    a. animated
    b. redundant
    c. inconsequential
    d. typical

WORDS IN CONTEXT

11. Her _____ nature meant that she never showed emotion even when terrible things kept happening to her.
   a. upsetting
   b. prestigious
   c. stoic
   d. sympathetic

12. The teacher put the crayons on the bottom shelf to make them _____ to the young children.
   a. accessible
   b. receptive
   c. eloquent
   d. ambiguous

13. My computer was state-of-the-art when I bought it five years ago, but now it is _____.
   a. current
   b. dedicated
   c. unnecessary
   d. outmoded

14. Lola had been traveling for weeks; she was on a _____ to find the perfect hotel.
   a. surge
   b. quest
   c. discovery
   d. cadence

15. Roland developed an _____ plan to earn extra money to buy the car he had always wanted.
   a. elitist
   b. irrational
   c. aloof
   d. ingenious

16. Jorge is _____ because he is the only one on staff who knows how to use this computer program.
   a. frustrated
   b. prudent
   c. indispensable
   d. creative

17. Selling ice-cold lemonade during a heat wave can be very _____.
   a. lucrative
   b. spiteful
   c. irrelevant
   d. revered

18. I do not like your negative attitude, and it has _____ affected our working relationship.
   a. favorably
   b. adversely
   c. shamelessly
   d. candidly

▶ Practice 2

Choose the word that best fills the blank in the following sentences. Check your answers at the end of the lesson.

1. It's easy to take care of my cousin's dog Sparky; he's a _____ and obedient pet.
   a. delectable
   b. commonplace
   c. meddlesome
   d. docile

WORDS IN CONTEXT

2. I had no trouble finding your house; your directions were _____.
   a. priceless
   b. arduous
   c. explicit
   d. embodied

3. Though the principal had expected an uproar when he canceled the senior class trip, both parents and students seemed _____.
   a. enraged
   b. apathetic
   c. suspicious
   d. evasive

4. Make sure that drinking water is _____; otherwise, you could get sick.
   a. valid
   b. quenchable
   c. impure
   d. potable

5. I will vote in favor of the new city ordinance because it _____ many of the points we discussed earlier this year.
   a. encompasses
   b. releases
   c. reminisces
   d. disperses

6. Rachel _____ a plan to become a millionaire by age thirty.
   a. devised
   b. conformed
   c. decreased
   d. condoned

7. Juana was known as a _____ person; she was always worrying about something.
   a. loquacious
   b. illogical
   c. fretful
   d. shrewd

8. The famous celebrity expected _____ treatment wherever she went.
   a. tepid
   b. consoling
   c. exorbitant
   d. preferential

9. Jessica needs an A in her class, so studying for exams takes _____ over watching television.
   a. precedence
   b. conformity
   c. perplexity
   d. endeavor

10. My mother was _____ when she discovered I broke her favorite vase.
   a. irate
   b. ironic
   c. indifferent
   d. obscure

11. Whitney fell asleep during the movie because it had a(n) _____ plot.
   a. monotonous
   b. torrid
   c. ample
   d. vital

WORDS IN CONTEXT

12. Barney _____ to go back to school to study dog grooming.
   a. relied
   b. surmised
   c. presumed
   d. resolved

13. Your drawing is a fair _____ of my family as the infamous Doppler gang.
   a. portrayal
   b. council
   c. desolation
   d. degeneration

14. When Marty let go of the handlebars, his bike _____ down the hill and splashed into a duck pond.
   a. dissented
   b. ventilated
   c. careened
   d. agitated

15. My sister decided to change her diet when the sour milk on her cereal gave off a _____ odor.
   a. pungent
   b. virtuous
   c. fraudulent
   d. frugal

16. The 5:00 whistle _____ announces the end of the workday at the largest toothpaste factory in town.
   a. approvingly
   b. significantly
   c. symbolically
   d. audibly

17. Jade was so hungry after her workout that she _____ gobbled up the fruit salad.
   a. dynamically
   b. voraciously
   c. generously
   d. beneficially

18. A small _____ occurred when my car door nicked the fender of a neighboring motor scooter.
   a. mishap
   b. attraction
   c. reflex
   d. duplicate

▶ Practice 3

Choose the word that best fills the blank in the following sentences. Check your answers at the end of the lesson.

1. Jose rose to a _____ sales position when he helped the company double its profits.
   a. average
   b. prominent
   c. prudent
   d. objective

2. Jeffrey was visibly nervous and spoke _____ about his upcoming appointment with his lawyer.
   a. warily
   b. luxuriously
   c. measurably
   d. narrowly

WORDS IN CONTEXT

3. The painter was a(n) _____ artist who was hardly known outside his native city.
   a. infamous
   b. stubborn
   c. eminent
   d. obscure

4. When Wayne learned that he had won the contest, he developed an _____ attitude, and we all had to listen to him crow about his accomplishments.
   a. arrogant
   b. achievable
   c. enlightened
   d. objective

5. Andrew showed _____ disregard for his pickup when he neglected to replenish the oil after the warning light came on.
   a. wanton
   b. admissive
   c. pretentious
   d. eloquent

6. Denise showed great _____ when she refused to discuss what was on the final exam in her economics class.
   a. substance
   b. generosity
   c. obligation
   d. integrity

7. The hail _____ the corn until the entire crop was lost.
   a. belittled
   b. pummeled
   c. rebuked
   d. commended

8. One of Angelo's _____ is collecting antique lemon juicers.
   a. eccentricities
   b. disappointments
   c. admonitions
   d. idioms

9. The motel offered a _____ after our long drive in the Grand Canyon.
   a. relapse
   b. respite
   c. brevity
   d. median

10. Margot brought large garbage bags to _____ our cleanup along Route 66.
    a. confound
    b. pacify
    c. integrate
    d. facilitate

11. Sandy's excellent bobsledding skills during the competition _____ what we all hoped to master.
    a. prevailed
    b. diverged
    c. exemplified
    d. varied

12. The _____ of sunshine and warm weather made for a happy vacation at the beach.
    a. assumption
    b. confluence
    c. seclusion
    d. treatise

13. Do you have the _____ papers to apply for this job?
    a. punitive
    b. grandiose
    c. restorative
    d. requisite

WORDS IN CONTEXT

14. Don't _____ yourself: You must pass that exam to graduate.
   a. delude
   b. depreciate
   c. relinquish
   d. prohibit

15. When you write your paper about *The Catcher in the Rye,* please be sure to give a _____ description of the main character.
   a. principled
   b. determined
   c. comprehensive
   d. massive

16. Although Maria was _____ when we first met her, she soon came to talk more than any of us.
   a. customary
   b. reticent
   c. animated
   d. voluntary

17. Viola thought that comparing fingerprints would be exciting work, but she actually found it quite _____.
   a. glamorous
   b. tedious
   c. dynamic
   d. prestigious

18. In some countries during the winter months, there is _____ darkness; the sun never rises.
   a. blinding
   b. brief
   c. perpetual
   d. offending

▶ Practice 4

Choose the word that best fills the blank in the following sentences. Check your answers at the end of the lesson.

1. After an hour of heavy rain, the storm _____ and we were able to get back out on the golf course.
   a. abated
   b. germinated
   c. constricted
   d. evoked

2. After years of experience, Layna became the _____ veterinarian, performing surgery with ease.
   a. acute
   b. superficial
   c. consummate
   d. ample

3. Anthony tended his neighbors' goldfish _____ while they were on vacation.
   a. terminally
   b. perpendicularly
   c. assiduously
   d. essentially

4. Her _____ business sense meant that she always made the best and most profitable decisions.
   a. erring
   b. radical
   c. shrewd
   d. subjective

WORDS IN CONTEXT

5. My friend _____ me by hugging me and making sure I was okay.
   a. intimidated
   b. consoled
   c. alienated
   d. stunned

6. The two cats could be _____ only by the number of rings on their tails; otherwise, they were exactly alike.
   a. separated
   b. divided
   c. disconnected
   d. differentiated

7. The room was _____, the bed unmade, and the dishes dirty; mice and cockroaches were everywhere.
   a. squalid
   b. squeamish
   c. queasy
   d. licentious

8. The drive was dangerous because of the rain; on each slick, wet curve I was afraid we would _____ into a ditch.
   a. operate
   b. hydroplane
   c. submerge
   d. reconnoiter

9. Eduardo liked to _____ his younger sister and make her upset.
   a. provoke
   b. upgrade
   c. spoil
   d. heave

10. Yelena was always _____ with her money; she preferred to save it than spend it.
   a. wistful
   b. desultory
   c. expository
   d. prudent

11. The tiny boat spun into the _____, and we were sure that all hope was lost.
   a. matrix
   b. paradox
   c. vector
   d. vortex

12. The old man was _____; he refused to leave his home, even when told the volcano was about to erupt.
   a. recitative
   b. redundant
   c. repatriated
   d. recalcitrant

13. The project seemed _____, so we all applied ourselves to it with enthusiasm.
   a. implacable
   b. feasible
   c. incorrigible
   d. irreparable

14. The many colors in the swarm of butterflies seemed to create a(n) _____ cloud.
   a. incandescent
   b. iridescent
   c. luminescent
   d. cumulous

WORDS IN CONTEXT

15. Mike and Jamal had a perfect _____, each seeming to know, without being told, what the other felt.
  a. stability
  b. equilibrium
  c. rapport
  d. symmetry

16. I always relied on the manager to _____ a new project when productivity was low.
  a. oppose
  b. induct
  c. instigate
  d. transpose

17. Now that she is a teenager, my daughter is _____ to talk about virtually all personal topics—she simply sits and stares at me.
  a. synchronous
  b. unanimous
  c. indentured
  d. reticent

18. *The New York Times* printed an erroneous report about New York City student scores on standardized tests, so the school board demanded a(n) _____.
  a. abolition
  b. invalidation
  c. retraction
  d. annulment

19. I expected the so-called bully to be mean, but he was actually quite _____.
  a. acerbic
  b. amiable
  c. vitriolic
  d. caustic

▶ Practice 5

Choose the word that best fills the blank in the following sentences. For each sentence you will have a pair of words to choose from. The pairs contain words that are easily confused and commonly misused.

1. Janelle _____ first aid to the child with the broken arm.
  a. administered
  b. ministered

2. Enrique was _____ to see his kids after his long vacation.
  a. eager
  b. anxious

3. The judge set a huge amount for bail to _____ that the man would return to court.
  a. ensure
  b. insure

4. I turned green and became _____ after I rode the Super Loops ten times.
  a. nauseous
  b. nauseated

5. She looks fabulous in that dress; it fits _____.
  a. good
  b. well

6. The United States is _____ of 50 states.
  a. composed
  b. comprised

7. If I lose all of my savings, I will be profoundly _____.
  a. discomfited
  b. discomforted

WORDS IN CONTEXT

8. All of the police officers were _____ witnesses because they actually saw the accident.
   a. credible
   b. credulous

9. When I cheat on my diet by eating chocolate cake, I have a guilty _____.
   a. conscious
   b. conscience

10. Dogs _____ to the cold weather when their fur grows thick.
   a. adapt
   b. adopt

11. A vitamin a day is part of a _____ diet.
   a. healthy
   b. healthful

12. After his amazing career, it seemed time to _____ him into the hall of fame.
   a. deduct
   b. induct

13. This book is an _____ study of the Mayan culture.
   a. exhaustive
   b. exhausting

14. Because she lived across the globe, it was not _____ for Latania to attend her high school reunion.
   a. feasible
   b. possible

15. The mail carrier _____ puts my neighbor's mail in my box.
   a. continuously
   b. continually

16. We will _____ with the plan we made earlier this month.
   a. proceed
   b. precede

17. Before buying a house, you should seek the _____ of a qualified attorney.
   a. counsel
   b. council

18. In most classes, homework is _____.
   a. compulsive
   b. compulsory

19. Her students appreciate Professor Diamond's _____ grading system.
   a. judicial
   b. judicious

20. He spoke _____ so everyone could hear.
   a. aloud
   b. allowed

▶ Answers

Practice 1

1. **d.** The word *problem* in this context means a source of distress. Choices **b** and **c** do not make sense. Choice **a** is a great source of distress, but parking tickets are usually not a disaster.
2. **c.** *Rescue* in this context implies freeing from danger. The other choices do not make sense.
3. **d.** *Considerable* means large. You would expect a brand new sports car to cost a lot of money.
4. **b.** The context clue is "we knew nothing." *Secretive* means having the habit of keeping secrets.
5. **b.** *Summit* means the highest point, where the hikers would have a view.

WORDS IN CONTEXT

6. **c.** A *consequence* is the result of something.
7. **c.** A *musty* odor is one that is stale or moldy. The other choices are not descriptive of an odor.
8. **a.** *Solitude*, unlike *loneliness* (choice **c**), can be a desirable thing. It's doubtful that a person who dealt with *crowds of noisy, demanding people* every day would want *association* (choice **b**). Choice **d** makes no sense.
9. **b.** To be *shunned* is to be avoided deliberately, usually as a punishment.
10. **b.** *Redundant* means repetitive. It is repetitive to describe a blackbird as black.
11. **c.** *Stoic* means not affected by emotion.
12. **a.** *Accessible* means capable of being reached; being within reach.
13. **d.** *Outmoded* means no longer in style or no longer usable.
14. **b.** A *quest* is a search or pursuit of something.
15. **d.** *Ingenious* means marked by originality, resourcefulness, and cleverness in conception; clever.
16. **c.** To be *indispensable* is to be essential or necessary.
17. **a.** *Lucrative* means profitable.
18. **b.** *Adversely* means acting against or in a contrary direction.

Practice 2

1. **d.** *Docile* means easily led or managed.
2. **c.** *Explicit* means clearly defined.
3. **b.** *Apathetic* means having little or no concern. (The principal had expected an uproar, but that never happened.)
4. **d.** *Potable* means fit for drinking.
5. **a.** *Encompasses* in this context means includes.
6. **a.** *Devised* means to form in the mind by new combinations or applications of ideas or principles; to plan to obtain or bring about.
7. **c.** *Fretful* means worried.
8. **d.** *Preferential* means special.

9. **a.** *Precedence* means priority of importance—i.e., studying is more important to Jessica than watching television.
10. **a.** *Irate* means upset or angry. You would expect someone to be irate if a favorite possession were destroyed.
11. **a.** *Monotonous* means having a tedious sameness.
12. **d.** *Resolved* means having reached a firm decision about something.
13. **a.** *Portrayal* means representation or portrait.
14. **c.** *Careen* means to rush headlong or carelessly; to lurch or swerve while in motion.
15. **a.** *Pungent* implies a sharp, stinging, or biting quality, especially of an odor.
16. **d.** *Audibly* means the manner of being heard.
17. **b.** *Voraciously* means ravenously.
18. **a.** *Mishap* means an unfortunate accident.

Practice 3

1. **b.** *Prominent* means important or leading.
2. **a.** *Warily* means in a manner marked by keen caution, cunning, or watchful prudence. The context clue in this sentence is Jeffrey's nervousness.
3. **d.** *Obscure* means unknown.
4. **a.** *Arrogant* means exaggerating or disposed to exaggerate one's own worth or importance in an overbearing manner.
5. **a.** *Wanton* means being without check or limitation.
6. **d.** *Integrity* means firm adherence to a code of moral values; honesty.
7. **b.** To *pummel* means to pound or beat.
8. **a.** An *eccentricity* is something that deviates from the norm. (Antique lemon juicers are not a commonplace item.)
9. **b.** *Respite* means an interval of rest and relief.
10. **d.** *Facilitate* means to make easier or to help bring about.
11. **c.** *Exemplify* means to be an instance of or serve as an example.

12. **b.** *Confluence* means a coming or flowing together, meeting, or gathering at one point.
13. **d.** *Requisite* means essential or necessary.
14. **a.** *Delude* means to mislead the mind; to deceive.
15. **c.** *Comprehensive* means covering completely or broadly. (*Massive*, choice **d**, refers to a large or bulky mass.)
16. **b.** *Reticent* means inclined to be silent or uncommunicative; reserved. Maria was silent at first, but then talked more than anyone else.
17. **b.** *Tedious* means tiresome or boring.
18. **c.** *Perpetual* means unending.

Practice 4

1. **a.** *Abated* means to decrease in force or intensity.
2. **c.** *Consummate* (adj.) means extremely skilled and experienced.
3. **c.** *Assiduously* means in a careful manner or with unremitting attention.
4. **c.** *Shrewd* means clever.
5. **b.** *Console* means to comfort.
6. **d.** To *differentiate* between two things is to establish the distinction between them. The other choices, although somewhat related, make no sense.
7. **a.** Something *squalid* has a dirty or wretched appearance. The other adjectives, though somewhat related, can properly be applied to a person but not to a place.
8. **b.** When a car goes out of control and skims along the surface of a wet road, it is called *hydroplaning*.
9. **a.** *Provoke* means to cause anger.
10. **d.** *Prudent* means cautious.
11. **d.** A *vortex* is a whirlpool and so fits the sentence. The other choices do not make sense.
12. **d.** To be *recalcitrant* is to be stubbornly resistant.
13. **b.** To be *feasible* is to be practicable and so the word best fits this sentence. The other three choices would not apply to projects that are possible (note that they all begin with prefixes generally meaning "not").
14. **b.** Something that is *iridescent* displays lustrous, rainbow colors. Choices **a** and **b** are somewhat close, but neither necessarily includes color as a necessary property. *Cumulous* (choice **d**) is a scientific name for a type of cloud.
15. **c.** To have *rapport* is to have mutual trust and emotional affinity. The other words do not necessarily imply trust.
16. **c.** *Instigate* means to cause or start.
17. **d.** To be *reticent* is to be disinclined to speak out. The other choices make no sense in this context.
18. **c.** To *retract* something is to take it back or disavow it. This is the term usually applied to disavowing something erroneous or libelous printed in a newspaper. The other choices are somewhat similar in meaning but do not normally apply to newspaper errors.
19. **b.** *Amiable* means friendly. Although the sentence is talking about a bully, the key word *but* indicates that the quality he has is not expected.

Practice 5

1. **a.** To *administer* means to give something remedially (transitive verb). To *minister* means to aid or give service to people (intransitive verb).
2. **a.** *Eager* implies enthusiastic or impatient desire or interest. *Anxious* implies a more negative feeling: an extreme uneasiness of mind, or worried.
3. **a.** *Ensure* means to make a future occurrence certain or reliable; *insure* means protecting the worth of goods; *assure* means to promise or cause someone to count on.
4. **b.** *Nauseated* means to feel nausea or the condition of feeling sick. *Nauseous* means causing nausea; nauseating; sickening. If you say

WORDS IN CONTEXT

you are nauseous it means you have unpleasant powers.

5. b. *Well* should be used as an adverb to modify verbs (how does it fit?). *Good* is an adjective often used with linking verbs (*be, seem,* or *appea*r).

6. b. *Comprised* means to consist of—it expresses the relation of the larger to the smaller (think of this larger sense by remembering that *comprised* is a longer word than composes). *Composed* means to make up the parts of.

7. a. *Discomfit* means to wholly undo or defeat. *Discomfort* means to deprive of comfort or to distress.

8. a. *Credible* means offering reasonable grounds for being believed; *credulous* means ready to believe, especially on slight or uncertain evidence.

9. b. *Conscience* means a sense of moral goodness. *Conscious* means alert or aware.

10. a. *Adapt* implies a modification according to changing circumstances. *Adopt* means accepting something created by another or foreign to one's nature.

11. b. *Healthful* implies a positive contribution to a healthy condition, or beneficial to health. *Healthy* implies full of strength and vigor as well as freedom from signs of disease.

12. b. *Induct* means to introduce or initiate. *Deduct* means to take away from a total.

13. a. *Exhaustive* means treating all parts without omission. *Exhausting* means tiring.

14. a. *Feasible* means logical or likely. *Possible* means capable of happening or existing.

15. b. *Continually* means recurring regularly. *Continuously* means uninterrupted in time.

16. a. *Proceed* means to go forward in an orderly way; *precede* means to come before.

17. a. *Counsel* means advice or guidance. A *council* is an assembly of people called together for consultation.

18. b. *Compulsory* means obligatory or required. *Compulsive* means having the capacity to compel.

19. b. *Judicious* is having or exhibiting sound judgment. *Judicial* is of, or relating to, courts of law.

20. a. *Aloud* means able to be heard. *Allowed* means permitted.

CHAPTER 14 ▶ Synonyms and Antonyms

A word is a **synonym** of another word if it has *the same or nearly the same* meaning as the word to which it is being compared. An **antonym** is a word that means *the opposite* of the word to which it is being compared. Questions on the ASVAB often ask you to find the synonym or antonym of a word. Sometimes the word will be in context—surrounded by a sentence that helps you guess what the word means. Other times, you will be provided with only the word and will have to decipher what the word means without help from the context.

▶ Synonyms

Questions that ask for synonyms can be tricky because they require you to recognize the meanings of several words that may be unfamiliar to you—not only the words in the question, but also the words in the answer choices. Usually, the best strategy is to look at the structure of the word and listen for its sound. See if a part of a word looks familiar. Think of other words you know that may have similar key elements, and then think about how those words could be related.

SYNONYMS AND ANTONYMS

▶ Practice 1

For each question, choose the synonym. Check your answers at the end of the lesson.

1. Which word means the same as ENTHUSIASTIC?
   a. adamant
   b. available
   c. cheerful
   d. eager

2. Which word means the same as ADEQUATE?
   a. sufficient
   b. awful
   c. proficient
   d. stupendous

3. Which word means the same as ECSTATIC?
   a. inconsistent
   b. positive
   c. wild
   d. thrilled

4. Which word means the same as AFFECT?
   a. accomplish
   b. conflict
   c. sicken
   d. influence

5. Which word means the same as CONTINUOUS?
   a. intermittent
   b. adjacent
   c. uninterrupted
   d. contiguous

6. Which word means the same as COURTESY?
   a. civility
   b. congruity
   c. conviviality
   d. rudeness

7. Which word means the same as DAINTY?
   a. vivid
   b. delicate
   c. robust
   d. adaptable

8. Which word means the same as RECUPERATE?
   a. mend
   b. endorse
   c. persist
   d. worsen

9. Which word means the same as PEACEFUL?
   a. majestic
   b. scarce
   c. tranquil
   d. adequate

10. Which word means the same as COMPOSURE?
    a. agitation
    b. poise
    c. liveliness
    d. stimulation

11. Which word means the same as STRIFE?
    a. conflict
    b. strange
    c. remove
    d. achieve

12. Which word means the same as COMMENDABLE?
    a. admirable
    b. accountable
    c. irresponsible
    d. noticeable

13. Which word means the same as PASSIVE?
    a. inactive
    b. emotional
    c. lively
    d. woeful

SYNONYMS AND ANTONYMS

14. Which word means the same as VAST?
   a. attentive
   b. immense
   c. steady
   d. slight

15. Which word means the same as COMPLY?
   a. subdue
   b. entertain
   c. flatter
   d. obey

16. Which word means the same as WILL?
   a. resolve
   b. spite
   c. sanity
   d. idleness

17. Which word means the same as ENLIGHTEN?
   a. relocate
   b. confuse
   c. comply
   d. teach

18. Which word means the same as RIGOROUS?
   a. demanding
   b. tolerable
   c. lenient
   d. disorderly

19. Which word means the same as OBLIVIOUS?
   a. visible
   b. sinister
   c. conscious
   d. unaware

20. Which word means the same as VERIFY?
   a. disclose
   b. confirm
   c. refute
   d. unite

▶ Practice 2

For each question, choose the synonym. Check your answers at the end of the lesson.

1. Which word means the same as ERRONEOUS?
   a. digressive
   b. confused
   c. impenetrable
   d. incorrect

2. Which word means the same as GROTESQUE?
   a. extreme
   b. frenzied
   c. hideous
   d. typical

3. Which word means the same as GARBLED?
   a. lucid
   b. unintelligible
   c. devoured
   d. outrageous

4. Which word means the same as PUNGENT?
   a. odorous
   b. puerile
   c. aware
   d. sharp

5. Which word means the same as COERCE?
   a. force
   b. permit
   c. waste
   d. deny

6. Which word means the same as ABRUPT?
   a. interrupt
   b. sudden
   c. extended
   d. corrupt

SYNONYMS AND ANTONYMS

7. Which word means the same as APATHY?
   a. hostility
   b. depression
   c. indifference
   d. concern

8. Which word means the same as DISPARAGE?
   a. disparate
   b. degrade
   c. dispose
   d. parry

9. Which word means the same as CONTEMPTUOUS?
   a. respectful
   b. unique
   c. scornful
   d. insecure

10. Which word means the same as TOTE?
   a. acquire
   b. carry
   c. tremble
   d. abandon

11. Which word means the same as DISTINCT?
   a. satisfied
   b. frenzied
   c. uneasy
   d. separate

12. Which word means the same as FLAGRANT?
   a. secret
   b. worthless
   c. noble
   d. glaring

13. Which word means the same as ORATION?
   a. nuisance
   b. independence
   c. address
   d. length

14. Which word means the same as LIBEL?
   a. description
   b. praise
   c. destiny
   d. slander

15. Which word means the same as PHILANTHROPY?
   a. selfishness
   b. fascination
   c. disrespect
   d. generosity

16. Which word means the same as PROXIMITY?
   a. distance
   b. agreement
   c. nearness
   d. intelligence

17. Which word means the same as NEGLIGIBLE?
   a. insignificant
   b. delicate
   c. meaningful
   d. illegible

18. Which word means the same as VIGILANT?
   a. nonchalant
   b. watchful
   c. righteous
   d. strenuous

19. Which word means the same as ASTUTE?
   a. perceptive
   b. inattentive
   c. stubborn
   d. elegant

20. Which word means the same as COLLABORATE?
   a. cooperate
   b. coordinate
   c. entice
   d. elaborate

SYNONYMS AND ANTONYMS

▶ Practice 3

For each question, choose the word that has the same or nearly the same meaning as the capitalized word. Check your answers at the end of the lesson.

1. SUBSCRIBE
   a. sign
   b. read
   c. divide
   d. support

2. OPPORTUNITY
   a. sensitivity
   b. arrogance
   c. chance
   d. reference

3. INVENT
   a. insert
   b. discover
   c. apply
   d. allow

4. SPHERE
   a. air
   b. spread
   c. globe
   d. enclosure

5. REFINE
   a. condone
   b. provide
   c. change
   d. purify

6. NARRATE
   a. tell
   b. story
   c. concede
   d. participate

7. NULLIFY
   a. numb
   b. delete
   c. negate
   d. petrify

8. SAGE
   a. wise
   b. obnoxious
   c. conceited
   d. heartless

9. URBANE
   a. city
   b. sophisticated
   c. unnerved
   d. rural

10. DORMANT
    a. hidden
    b. slumbering
    c. rigid
    d. misplaced

11. BANISH
    a. exile
    b. decorate
    c. succumb
    d. encourage

12. TAILOR
    a. measure
    b. construct
    c. launder
    d. alter

13. WAIVE
    a. merge
    b. relinquish
    c. destroy
    d. hinder

SYNONYMS AND ANTONYMS

14. EVADE
 a. cause
 b. avoid
 c. remind
 d. destroy

15. ETERNAL
 a. timeless
 b. heavenly
 c. loving
 d. wealthy

16. TIMID
 a. shy
 b. terrific
 c. terrified
 d. forgetful

17. STOW
 a. pack
 b. curtsy
 c. fool
 d. trample

18. REVOKE
 a. affect
 b. condone
 c. condemn
 d. annul

19. COVERT
 a. change
 b. hidden
 c. movement
 d. mission

20. FALTER
 a. falsify
 b. determine
 c. stumble
 d. plague

▶ **Practice 4**

Choose the word that means the same or nearly the same as the underlined word. Check your answers at the end of the lesson.

1. its <u>inferior</u> quality
 a. noted
 b. distinguished
 c. lower
 d. questionable

2. in a <u>curt</u> manner
 a. gruff
 b. careful
 c. devious
 d. calm

3. their <u>perilous</u> journey
 a. dangerous
 b. doubtful
 c. adventurous
 d. thrilling

4. the <u>precise</u> amount
 a. fair
 b. exact
 c. undetermined
 d. valuable

5. to <u>commence</u> the meeting
 a. begin
 b. leave
 c. disclose
 d. terminate

6. a <u>humble</u> person
 a. common
 b. tolerant
 c. conceited
 d. unassertive

SYNONYMS AND ANTONYMS

7. a <u>jubilant</u> graduate
   a. charming
   b. joyful
   c. stubborn
   d. scholarly

8. created a <u>replica</u>
   a. portion
   b. masterpiece
   c. prompt
   d. copy

9. a <u>temperate</u> climate
   a. moderate
   b. harsh
   c. warm
   d. cold

10. a <u>destitute</u> person
   a. poor
   b. wise
   c. traveling
   d. large

11. the <u>agile</u> dancer
   a. proud
   b. nimble
   c. humble
   d. talented

12. acted <u>brazenly</u>
   a. boldly
   b. blissfully
   c. brutally
   d. broadly

13. the <u>unique</u> individual
   a. rigorous
   b. admirable
   c. unparalleled
   d. remarkable

14. the <u>prerequisite</u> number of items
   a. optional
   b. preferred
   c. advisable
   d. required

15. <u>alleviate</u> the pain
   a. ease
   b. tolerate
   c. stop
   d. intensify

16. an <u>ample</u> supply
   a. meager
   b. archaic
   c. generous
   d. paltry

17. the <u>unanimous</u> decision
   a. uniform
   b. divided
   c. adamant
   d. clear-cut

18. the <u>proficient</u> worker
   a. inexperienced
   b. unequaled
   c. sufficient
   d. skilled

19. <u>obstinately</u> refused
   a. repeatedly
   b. reluctantly
   c. angrily
   d. stubbornly

20. to <u>rectify</u> the situation
   a. correct
   b. forget
   c. alter
   d. abuse

▶ Practice 5

Choose the word that means the same or nearly the same as the underlined word. Check your answers at the end of the lesson.

1. expedite the process
   a. accelerate
   b. evaluate
   c. reverse
   d. justify

2. a fictitious character
   a. evil
   b. imaginary
   c. prominent
   d. colorful

3. to absolve a person
   a. convict
   b. accuse
   c. forgive
   d. exclude

4. to hoist the flag
   a. lower
   b. destroy
   c. salute
   d. raise

5. to disrupt an event
   a. interrupt
   b. invent
   c. organize
   d. host

6. to sustain a cause
   a. demolish
   b. renovate
   c. support
   d. remodel

7. simmering anger
   a. unacknowledged
   b. diminishing
   c. righteous
   d. seething

8. to initiate a campaign
   a. support
   b. begin
   c. sabotage
   d. run

9. ravenous hunger
   a. natural
   b. ungratified
   c. voracious
   d. satisfied

10. uninhabitable island
    a. deserted
    b. unlivable
    c. remote
    d. uncivilized

11. suppressed anger
    a. explosive
    b. repressed
    c. minimized
    d. expressed

12. to be immersed in study
    a. trapped
    b. absorbed
    c. held
    d. enriched

13. to detract from something
    a. destroy
    b. break
    c. obliterate
    d. diminish

SYNONYMS AND ANTONYMS

14. to <u>haggle</u> over the price
   a. bargain
   b. complain
   c. worry
   d. cheat

15. <u>palpable</u> tension
   a. rising
   b. understated
   c. nervous
   d. tangible

16. a <u>solemn</u> ceremony
   a. impudent
   b. serious
   c. religious
   d. marriage

17. urban <u>sprawl</u>
   a. decay
   b. construction
   c. growth
   d. crime

18. an <u>ingenious</u> invention
   a. worthwhile
   b. credible
   c. clever
   d. desolate

19. a <u>meandering</u> stream
   a. clear
   b. flowing
   c. polluted
   d. winding

20. a <u>precarious</u> situation
   a. joyous
   b. dangerous
   c. unforgettable
   d. secure

▶ Antonyms

Many antonyms seem obvious—good and bad, night and day—but others are not as easily recognizable. This is because many words have more than one meaning. For example, the word *clear* could mean cloudless, transparent, or unmistakable. For each of those meanings, clear has an opposite. If an antonym isn't obvious, think about other possible meanings of the word. Also, do not be fooled by answer choices that are synonyms. Remember that you are looking for a word that means the *opposite*, not a word that means the same. You can check your answers at the end of the lesson.

▶ Practice 6

1. Which word means the *opposite* of UNITY?
   a. discord
   b. stimulation
   c. consent
   d. neglect

2. Which word means the *opposite* of DETEST?
   a. prohibit
   b. hate
   c. examine
   d. admire

3. Which word means the *opposite* of VALIANT?
   a. instinctive
   b. cowardly
   c. cynical
   d. worthy

4. Which word means the *opposite* of LENIENT?
   a. capable
   b. impractical
   c. merciful
   d. domineering

SYNONYMS AND ANTONYMS

5. Which word means the *opposite* of TARNISH?
   a. absorb
   b. endure
   c. shine
   d. sully

6. Which word means the *opposite* of CREDIBLE?
   a. unimportant
   b. conventional
   c. comparable
   d. unbelievable

7. Which word means the *opposite* of YIELD?
   a. merge
   b. offer
   c. resist
   d. provide

8. Which word means the *opposite* of COMMENCE?
   a. initiate
   b. adapt
   c. harass
   d. terminate

9. Which word means the *opposite* of CONSCIENTIOUS?
   a. careless
   b. apologetic
   c. diligent
   d. boisterous

10. Which word means the *opposite* of DEFICIENT?
   a. necessary
   b. complete
   c. flawed
   d. simple

11. Which word means the *opposite* of CLARIFY?
   a. explain
   b. dismay
   c. obscure
   d. provide

12. Which word means the *opposite* of GRANT?
   a. deny
   b. consume
   c. allocate
   d. provoke

13. Which word means the *opposite* of LUCID?
   a. ordinary
   b. turbulent
   c. implausible
   d. unclear

14. Which word means the *opposite* of IMPARTIAL?
   a. complete
   b. prejudiced
   c. unbiased
   d. erudite

15. Which word means the *opposite* of JUDICIOUS?
   a. partial
   b. litigious
   c. imprudent
   d. unrestrained

16. Which word means the *opposite* of SHALLOW?
   a. profound
   b. proficient
   c. ignorant
   d. malicious

17. Which word means the *opposite* of ERUDITE?
   a. uneducated
   b. polite
   c. unknown
   d. agitated

SYNONYMS AND ANTONYMS

18. Which word means the *opposite* of AMIABLE?
   a. dangerous
   b. permissive
   c. aloof
   d. congenial

19. Which word means the *opposite* of COMPETENT?
   a. incomplete
   b. intense
   c. inept
   d. massive

20. Which word means the *opposite* of PROMOTE?
   a. explicate
   b. curtail
   c. concede
   d. retain

▶ **Practice 7**

Choose the word that means the OPPOSITE or most nearly the opposite of the word in capitals.

1. DEPLETE
   a. remove
   b. replace
   c. diminish
   d. add

2. IRRITATE
   a. soothe
   b. drain
   c. resist
   d. solve

3. DECEITFUL
   a. honest
   b. deceptive
   c. misleading
   d. decrepit

4. VIRTUE
   a. reality
   b. fact
   c. vice
   d. amateur

5. HARMONY
   a. noise
   b. brevity
   c. safety
   d. discord

6. INSULT
   a. compliment
   b. contempt
   c. argument
   d. attitude

7. THRIVE
   a. divide
   b. fail
   c. recant
   d. diminish

8. SERENE
   a. severe
   b. diplomatic
   c. chaotic
   d. academic

9. DILIGENT
   a. serious
   b. sloppy
   c. elusive
   d. incredible

10. DEMOLISH
   a. attend
   b. consider
   c. create
   d. stifle

SYNONYMS AND ANTONYMS

11. NOTABLE
   a. oral
   b. graceful
   c. legal
   d. ordinary

12. BERATE
   a. tear
   b. replace
   c. inspect
   d. compliment

13. PROSPEROUS
   a. affluent
   b. destitute
   c. cowardly
   d. receptive

14. CONVENE
   a. scatter
   b. organize
   c. remit
   d. ignore

15. CRITICAL
   a. inimical
   b. judgmental
   c. massive
   d. trivial

16. NIMBLE
   a. sturdy
   b. sluggish
   c. thoughtless
   d. relaxed

17. TRANQUIL
   a. agitated
   b. explicit
   c. slow
   d. composed

18. SPRIGHTLY
   a. eagerly
   b. loftily
   c. dully
   d. locally

19. GENERATE
   a. elongate
   b. electrify
   c. destroy
   d. dignify

20. IMPULSIVE
   a. secure
   b. mandatory
   c. rash
   d. cautious

▶ Practice 8

Choose the word that means the OPPOSITE or most nearly the opposite of the word in capitals.

1. PRUDENT
   a. hasty
   b. licentious
   c. libertine
   d. demonstrative

2. RETAIN
   a. withhold
   b. release
   c. succumb
   d. incise

3. SCANT
   a. pellucid
   b. meager
   c. copious
   d. vocal

SYNONYMS AND ANTONYMS

4. KNOWLEDGEABLE
  a. bookish
  b. stubborn
  c. ignorant
  d. implied

5. STRINGENT
  a. obese
  b. lax
  c. obtuse
  d. fluid

6. COMMONPLACE
  a. incredulous
  b. mysterious
  c. boring
  d. solemn

7. SUCCINCT
  a. distinct
  b. laconic
  c. unpersuasive
  d. verbose

8. TIRESOME
  a. stimulating
  b. alarming
  c. intemperate
  d. tranquil

9. UNIFORM
  a. dissembling
  b. diverse
  c. bizarre
  d. slovenly

10. WARY
  a. alert
  b. leery
  c. worried
  d. careless

11. NOVEL
  a. dangerous
  b. unsettled
  c. suitable
  d. old

12. FALLACY
  a. truth
  b. blessing
  c. weakness
  d. fable

13. PERMANENT
  a. solid
  b. sober
  c. fleeting
  d. indifferent

14. SUBSEQUENT
  a. necessary
  b. insignificant
  c. primary
  d. previous

15. NONCHALANT
  a. intelligent
  b. popular
  c. concerned
  d. reckless

16. EXCISE
  a. sleep
  b. retain
  c. organize
  d. staple

17. DISPERSE
  a. gather
  b. agree
  c. praise
  d. satisfy

SYNONYMS AND ANTONYMS

18. PRESSING
  a. composed
  b. unimportant
  c. unlimited
  d. strong

19. MIRTH
  a. height
  b. solemnity
  c. expense
  d. preparation

20. SENSIBLE
  a. foolhardy
  b. replenished
  c. severe
  d. religious

▶ **Practice 9**

Choose the word that means the OPPOSITE or most nearly the opposite of the word in capitals.

1. ORIENT
  a. confuse
  b. arouse
  c. deter
  d. simplify

2. LEVITATE
  a. plod
  b. undulate
  c. whisper
  d. sink

3. PACIFY
  a. complicate
  b. dismiss
  c. excite
  d. atomize

4. PLAUSIBLE
  a. insufficient
  b. apologetic
  c. unbelievable
  d. credible

5. AVIDLY
  a. partially
  b. unenthusiastically
  c. equally
  d. unkindly

6. MEEKLY
  a. mildly
  b. painfully
  c. forcefully
  d. politely

7. COMPLACENT
  a. concerned
  b. pleasant
  c. happy
  d. convinced

8. AMBIGUOUS
  a. apathetic
  b. certain
  c. equivocal
  d. indefinite

9. SPONTANEOUS
  a. serious
  b. intimidated
  c. declarative
  d. prepared

10. ELOQUENT
  a. shabby
  b. fluent
  c. inarticulate
  d. plain

SYNONYMS AND ANTONYMS

11. DETERRENT
   a. encouragement
   b. obstacle
   c. proponent
   d. discomfort

12. ENTANGLE
   a. involve
   b. replace
   c. subject
   d. separate

13. IMPERTINENT
   a. animated
   b. rude
   c. relentless
   d. polite

14. LUDICROUS
   a. absurd
   b. somber
   c. reasonable
   d. charitable

15. ARCHAIC
   a. tangible
   b. modern
   c. ancient
   d. haunted

16. SULLEN
   a. morose
   b. impetuous
   c. provocative
   d. jovial

17. AWE
   a. contempt
   b. reverence
   c. valor
   d. distortion

18. TAUT
   a. neutral
   b. relaxed
   c. rigid
   d. vague

19. RILE
   a. appease
   b. prosper
   c. oppress
   d. irk

20. MAR
   a. delineate
   b. bolster
   c. clarify
   d. repair

▶ Practice 10

Choose the word that means the OPPOSITE or most nearly the opposite of the word in capitals.

1. INTREPID
   a. belligerent
   b. consistent
   c. chivalrous
   d. fearful

2. METHODICAL
   a. erratic
   b. deliberate
   c. hostile
   d. deformed

3. LATENT
   a. slow
   b. tardy
   c. dormant
   d. active

SYNONYMS AND ANTONYMS

4. AFFABLE
  a. disagreeable
  b. hollow
  c. simple
  d. eager

5. TREPIDATION
  a. distribution
  b. agitation
  c. fearlessness
  d. uniformity

6. AUSPICIOUS
  a. unpromising
  b. repulsive
  c. jealous
  d. inattentive

7. IDLE
  a. slow
  b. illegible
  c. busy
  d. lucky

8. FURTIVELY
  a. silently
  b. openly
  c. mildly
  d. quickly

9. ENTICE
  a. excite
  b. tempt
  c. express
  d. repel

10. ORNATE
  a. simple
  b. gorgeous
  c. dirty
  d. pleased

11. OSTENTATIOUS
  a. hilarious
  b. humble
  c. careful
  d. obnoxious

12. ENDORSE
  a. condemn
  b. recommend
  c. announce
  d. adopt

13. ACCEDE
  a. excel
  b. retard
  c. disapprove
  d. increase

14. FRAIL
  a. scared
  b. hardy
  c. child-like
  d. attentive

15. AMBIVALENCE
  a. compensation
  b. decisiveness
  c. enthusiasm
  d. devotion

16. DIVERGENT
  a. persuasive
  b. identical
  c. incomplete
  d. malicious

17. PENSIVE
  a. nervous
  b. prejudiced
  c. dizzy
  d. thoughtless

SYNONYMS AND ANTONYMS

18. DISCERNIBLE
  a. invisible
  b. recognizable
  c. paradoxical
  d. scornful

19. BLEMISHED
  a. speckled
  b. flawless
  c. productive
  d. absent

20. ABHOR
  a. scare
  b. surprise
  c. desire
  d. inspire

▶ Answers

Practice 1
1. **d.** *Enthusiastic* means eager or excited.
2. **a.** If something is *adequate*, it is sufficient.
3. **d.** A person who is *ecstatic* is thrilled or exhilarated.
4. **d.** To *affect* means to influence.
5. **c.** *Continuous* means marked by uninterrupted extension in space and time.
6. **a.** A *courtesy* implies being courteous or mannerly; it is civility.
7. **b.** A *dainty* person is delicate.
8. **a.** *Recuperate* means to heal; to mend.
9. **c.** *Peaceful* and *tranquil* both mean calm.
10. **b.** If you gain your *composure*, you have poise.
11. **a.** *Strife* means a struggle or conflict.
12. **a.** *Commendable* is the same as admirable.
13. **a.** *Passive* means not active.
14. **b.** *Vast* means very great in size; immense.
15. **d.** To *comply* is the same as to obey.
16. **a.** *Will* and *resolve* share the same meaning.
17. **d.** If you *enlighten* someone, you have taught them something.
18. **a.** If something is *rigorous*, it is demanding.
19. **d.** If you are *oblivious* to your surroundings, you are unaware of them.
20. **b.** To *verify* means to establish the truth or accuracy; to confirm.

Practice 2
1. **d.** *Erroneous* means inaccurate, or incorrect.
2. **c.** *Grotesque* means distorted, or hideous.
3. **b.** If something is *garbled*, it is jumbled or unintelligible.
4. **d.** *Pungent* means caustic or sharp. Do not be tempted by choice **a**—*pungent* is a word used to describe an odor.
5. **a.** To *coerce* means to dominate by force.
6. **b.** *Abrupt* means sudden, quick, or hasty.
7. **c.** *Apathy* means a lack of interest or concern; indifference.
8. **b.** *Disparage* means to lower in rank or degrade.
9. **c.** A *contemptuous* person is full of scorn.
10. **b.** To *tote* means to carry.
11. **d.** If something is *distinct* it is distinguishable, or separate.
12. **d.** *Flagrant* means glaring.
13. **c.** An *oration* is a speech; an address.
14. **d.** *Libel* and *slander* both refer to defaming someone.
15. **d.** *Philanthropy* is a noun that means goodwill toward fellow men; humanitarianism; generosity.
16. **c.** *Proximity* means nearness.
17. **a.** *Negligible* means of little consequence; insignificant.
18. **b.** *Vigilant* means watchful, especially to danger.
19. **a.** *Astute* and *perceptive* both mean having or showing a keen awareness.
20. **a.** To *collaborate* means to work jointly with others; to cooperate.

SYNONYMS AND ANTONYMS

Practice 3
1. **d.** One meaning of *subscribe* is to support.
2. **c.** An *opportunity* to do something is the same as a *chance* to do it.
3. **b.** *Invent* means to create or to *discover*.
4. **c.** *Sphere* and *globe* both mean ball or orb.
5. **d.** To *refine* and to *purify* both mean to remove impurities.
6. **a.** *Narrate* means to tell. Do not be fooled by choice **b**—you narrate a story, but narrate does not mean story.
7. **c.** *Nullify* means to negate.
8. **a.** *Sage* and *wise* both mean intelligent, perceptive.
9. **b.** *Urbane* means sophisticated.
10. **b.** *Dormant* and *slumbering* both mean sleeping.
11. **a.** To *banish* and to *exile* both mean to force to leave.
12. **d.** To *tailor* and to *alter* both mean to make something fit.
13. **b.** To *waive* and to *relinquish* both mean to give up.
14. **b.** *Evade* means to avoid.
15. **a.** *Eternal* and *timeless* both mean without end.
16. **a.** *Timid* means shy or lacking boldness.
17. **a.** To *stow* and to *pack* both mean to store away.
18. **d.** *Revoke* means to take back or annul.
19. **b.** *Covert* means hidden.
20. **c.** *Falter* means to stumble.

Practice 4
1. **c.** *Inferior* is lower in rank, quality, or importance.
2. **a.** *Curt* means in a rude or *gruff* manner.
3. **a.** *Perilous* means hazardous or dangerous.
4. **b.** *Precise* means exact.
5. **a.** *Commence* means begin.
6. **d.** Someone who is *humble* is unassertive.
7. **b.** *Jubilant* means joyful.
8. **d.** A *replica* is a close reproduction; a copy or duplicate.
9. **a.** *Temperate* means not extreme or excessive; *moderate* means avoiding extremes of behavior or expression.
10. **a.** *Destitute* means lacking possessions and resources.
11. **b.** *Agile* means marked by ready ability to move with quick and easy grace; *nimble* means quick and light in motion.
12. **a.** *Brazenly* means marked by contemptuous boldness.
13. **c.** *Unique* means being the only one of its kind; *unparalleled* means unequaled.
14. **d.** To be a *prerequisite* is to be required; to be *required* is to be needed.
15. **a.** To *alleviate* is to make more bearable; to *ease* is to minimize difficulty.
16. **c.** *Ample* means generous or more than adequate.
17. **a.** *Unanimous* means in complete assent or agreement; *uniform* means unvarying or the same as another or others.
18. **d.** To be *proficient* is to be expert or adept at something; to be *skilled* is to show ability or expertness.
19. **d.** *Obstinately* means refractory or stubborn; *stubbornly* means unduly determined, not easily persuaded.
20. **a.** To *rectify* is to set something right; to *correct* is to remove errors from something.

Practice 5
1. **a.** *Expedite* means accelerate the process; to speed up.
2. **b.** *Fictitious* means imaginary.
3. **c.** To *absolve* means to exonerate or forgive; to free from blame or responsibility.
4. **d.** *Hoist* means to raise.
5. **a.** *Disrupt* means to interrupt or to disturb.
6. **c.** To *sustain* means to support.
7. **d.** *Simmering* means barely controlled; seething.
8. **b.** To *initiate* means to begin or cause to begin.
9. **c.** *Ravenous* means voracious, all-consuming.
10. **b.** *Uninhabitable* implies conditions are so terrible that life cannot be sustained there.

SYNONYMS AND ANTONYMS

11. **b.** *Suppressed* means held in, repressed, not expressed outwardly.
12. **b.** To be *immersed* means to be absorbed, engrossed, or involved in profoundly.
13. **d.** *Detract* means to diminish the importance of something.
14. **a.** *Haggle* means to bargain.
15. **d.** A *palpable* tension is so intense it almost seems to be a physical, tangible presence.
16. **b.** *Solemn* means serious.
17. **c.** One meaning of *sprawl* is haphazard growth of a city, usually outward toward the suburbs.
18. **c.** *Ingenious* means original or clever.
19. **d.** To *meander* means to follow a winding course.
20. **b.** *Precarious* means dangerous.

Practice 6

1. **a.** *Unity* means harmony or compatibility; *discord* means a lack of harmony.
2. **d.** *Detest* means to feel hostility toward, to strongly dislike; the opposite of detest is *admire*.
3. **b.** *Valiant* means acting with bravery or boldness; *cowardly* is the opposite.
4. **d.** *Lenient* means permissive, tolerant, or easygoing; *domineering* means exercising overbearing control.
5. **c.** *Tarnish* means to destroy the luster of; *shine* means to make bright by polishing.
6. **d.** *Credible* means believable; choice **d** is the opposite.
7. **c.** *Yield* means to submit; *resist* is the opposite.
8. **d.** *Commence* means to begin; *terminate* means to end.
9. **a.** *Conscientious* means careful, cautious, and thoughtful; *careless* means not showing care.
10. **b.** *Deficient* means lacking some necessary quality; *complete* means having all necessary parts.
11. **c.** *Clarify* means to make clear; *obscure* means to make dark, dim, or indistinct.

12. **a.** To *grant* is to permit; to *deny* is to refuse to permit.
13. **d.** *Lucid* means clear.
14. **b.** *Impartial* means not partial or biased; *prejudiced* means biased.
15. **c.** *Judicious* means wise or prudent; *imprudent* means not prudent.
16. **a.** *Shallow* means having very little depth of feeling; *profound* is the opposite.
17. **a.** *Erudite* means learned or possessing knowledge; *uneducated* means to lack training or knowledge.
18. **c.** *Amiable* means friendly; the opposite of friendly is *aloof*.
19. **c.** *Competent* means having adequate abilities; *inept* means incapable or not competent.
20. **b.** To *promote* is to advance someone to a higher rank or to advocate something; to *curtail* is to cut something short.

Practice 7

1. **d.** *Deplete* means to lessen; *add* is the opposite.
2. **a.** To *irritate* means to annoy; to *soothe* means to calm.
3. **a.** *Deceitful* means deceptive; *honest* is the opposite.
4. **c.** *Virtue* means a moral goodness; *vice* means a moral failing.
5. **d.** *Harmony* means agreement; *discord* means disagreement.
6. **a.** An *insult* is a gross indignity; a *compliment* is an admiring remark.
7. **b.** *Thrive* means to succeed; *fail* is the opposite.
8. **c.** *Serene* means calm; *chaotic* is the opposite.
9. **b.** *Diligent* means painstaking; *sloppy* is the opposite.
10. **c.** To *demolish* means to tear apart; to *create* means to build.
11. **d.** *Notable* means unusual; *ordinary* means usual.

SYNONYMS AND ANTONYMS

12. d. *Berate* means to scold; *compliment* is the opposite.
13. b. *Prosperous* means rich or affluent; *destitute* means very poor.
14. a. *Convene* means to gather; *scatter* is the opposite.
15. d. To be *critical* is to be important or vital to something; to be *trivial* is to be unimportant.
16. b. *Nimble* means quick and light in motion; *sluggish* means slow or inactive.
17. a. *Tranquil* means peaceful; *agitated* means disturbed or excited.
18. c. *Sprightly* means lively; *dully* suggests a lack or loss of keenness or zest.
19. c. *Generate* means to produce; *destroy* is the opposite.
20. d. To be *impulsive* is to be swayed by emotion or to make rash decisions; to be *cautious* is to show forethought.

Practice 8

1. a. To be *prudent* is to exercise good judgment; to be *hasty* is to show a lack of thought.
2. b. To *retain* is to keep or hold; to *release* is to let go.
3. c. *Scant* is meager; *copious* is abundant.
4. c. *Knowledgeable* means intelligent; *ignorant* is the opposite.
5. b. To be *stringent* is to be rigorous or severe; to be *lax* is to be lacking in rigor or strictness.
6. b. *Commonplace* means normal or typical; *mysterious* is the opposite.
7. d. To be *succinct* is to be concise; to be *verbose* is to be wordy.
8. a. To be *tiresome* is to be boring; to be *stimulating* is to be exciting.
9. b. To be *uniform* is to be consistent or the same as another or others; to be *diverse* is to have variety.
10. d. To be *wary* is to be on guard or watchful; *careless* is the opposite of watchful.

11. d. The adjective *novel* means new or not representing something formerly known; the adjective *old* means having lived or existed for a long time.
12. a. A *fallacy* is a false or mistaken idea, or trickery; a *truth* is something which conforms to the facts.
13. c. *Permanent* means everlasting; *fleeting* is the opposite.
14. d. *Subsequent* means coming after or following; *previous* means coming before.
15. c. To be *nonchalant* means to have an air of easy indifference; to be *concerned* means to be interested and involved.
16. b. To *excise* means to remove; to *retain* means to keep.
17. a. To *disperse* means to scatter; to *gather* means to collect in one place.
18. b. *Pressing* means urgent; *unimportant* is the opposite.
19. b. *Mirth* means merriment; *solemnity* means seriousness.
20. a. *Sensible* means reasonable; *foolhardy* is the opposite.

Practice 9

1. a. To *orient* means to adjust to; to *confuse* means to mix-up.
2. d. To *levitate* means to rise and float; to *sink* means to go under the surface.
3. c. To *pacify* means to calm; to *excite* means to stir up.
4. c. To be *plausible* is to be likely; to be *unbelievable* is to be unlikely.
5. b. *Avidly* means characterized by enthusiasm and vigorous pursuit.
6. c. *Meekly* means not violent or strong; *forcefully* means powerfully.
7. a. *Complacent* means self-satisfied or unconcerned.
8. b. To be *ambiguous* is to be equivocal or obscure; to be *certain* is to be definite or fixed.

SYNONYMS AND ANTONYMS

9. **d.** *Spontaneous* means impulsive or without planning; *prepared* is the opposite.
10. **c.** To be *eloquent* is to be fluent; to be *inarticulate* is to be unable to speak with clarity.
11. **a.** A *deterrent* prevents or discourages; *encouragement* inspires or heartens.
12. **d.** *Entangle* means to twist together; *separate* is the opposite.
13. **d.** Someone who is *impertinent* is rude; someone who is *polite* is courteous.
14. **c.** To be *ludicrous* is to be absurd; to be *reasonable* is to be rational.
15. **b.** To be *archaic* is to be ancient or outdated; to be *modern* is to be up to date.
16. **d.** *Sullen* means gloomy or dismal; *jovial* means very happy.
17. **a.** To be in *awe* of something is to admire it; to have *contempt* for something is to consider it worthless.
18. **b.** *Taut* means extremely tight; *relaxed* means not tense.
19. **a.** To *rile* is to upset; to *appease* is to pacify or satisfy.
20. **d.** To *mar* is to damage or deface; to *repair* is to restore or fix.

Practice 10

1. **d.** An *intrepid* person approaches a challenge without fear, which is the opposite of *fearful*.
2. **a.** *Methodical* means careful or in a planned manner; *erratic* means having no fixed course.
3. **d.** *Latent* means present but not active; *active* is the opposite.
4. **a.** *Affable* means pleasant and at ease; agreeable.
5. **c.** *Trepidation* means fear; the opposite would be *fearlessness*.
6. **a.** *Auspicious* means something taken as a sign promising success; the opposite is *unpromising*.
7. **c.** *Idle* means inactive; *busy* is the opposite.
8. **b.** *Furtively* means done stealthily or secretively.
9. **d.** *Entice* means to attract by arousing hope; *repel* means to drive away.
10. **a.** *Ornate* means highly decorated; *simple* is the opposite.
11. **b.** To be *ostentatious* is to be showy and boastful; the opposite would be *humble*.
12. **a.** *Endorse* means to approve; *condemn* means to disapprove.
13. **c.** *Accede* means to express approval or give consent; *disapprove* means to express disapproval.
14. **b.** *Frail* means weak; *hardy* is the opposite.
15. **b.** *Ambivalence* is uncertainty as to which approach to follow; *decisiveness* is having the power or quality of deciding.
16. **b.** *Divergent* means differing from a standard; *identical* means being the same.
17. **d.** *Pensive* means sadly thoughtful; *thoughtless* means lacking concern for others, careless, or devoid of thought.
18. **a.** One definition of *discernible* is visible with the eyes, so the opposite would be *invisible*.
19. **b.** *Blemished* means having marks or flaws; *flawless* is the opposite.
20. **c.** *Abhor* means to regard with repugnance; *desire* means to long for or hope for.

NOTES

NOTES

NOTES

NOTES

NOTES

Special FREE Offer from LearningExpress!

Let LearningExpress help you prepare for, and score higher on, the ASVAB

Go to the LearningExpress Practice Center at www.LearningExpressFreeOffer.com, an interactive online resource exclusively for LearningExpress customers.

Now that you've purchased LearningExpress's *ASVAB Success, 2nd Edition*, you have **FREE** access to:

- **Over 100 practice questions** that mirror the official ASVAB Core exam
- **Targeted practice** in arithmetic reasoning, mathematics, paragraph comprehension, and word knowledge
- **Immediate scoring** and **detailed answer explanations**
- Benchmark your skills and focus your study with our **customized diagnostic report**

Follow the simple instructions on the scratch card in your copy of *ASVAB Success, 2nd Edition*. Use your individualized access code found on the scratch card and go to www.LearningExpressFreeOffer.com to sign in. Start practicing online for the ASVAB right away!

Once you've logged on, use the spaces below to write in your access code and newly created password for easy reference:

Access Code: _____   Password: _____